D1302234

PRAISE FOR VISIONARIE$ ARE MADE NOT BORN

"Whether you aspire to lead a big organization, a start-up or anything in between, you must read *Visionarie$ are Made Not Born*. It will improve your perspective and approach."

Norman Bobins, Non-executive Chairman, The Private Bank; Former CEO, LaSalle Bank

"Lloyd Shefsky's effortless story telling opens up doors to some of the country's great business minds, in a way that makes us feel like we've been there right alongside him, enjoying the same cup of extra strong coffee for which he is famed. Reading these chapters reminds me that Lloyd has a gift for bouncing between strategy and tactics. A great read for anyone who spends their days striking the balance between operational effectiveness and long-term multi-generational strategy."

Garvin Brown, Chairman, Brown-Forman Corporation

"During my thirty seven years in the private equity business I have been involved with a number of true visionaries but I never analyzed what made them so. Lloyd Shefsky has nailed it, clearly describing the elements of vision and how they apply through his fascinating profiles of thirteen successful visionaries. I could not put this book down."

John Canning, Founder and Chairman, Madison Dearborn Partners

"The stories are great and superbly told. The lessons are profound, providing a whole new way of looking at how business visionaries do their thing, explained in ways we all can emulate. Don't miss *Visionarie$ are Made Not Born*. It's a great book to give to a rising entrepreneur, friend, colleague or family member!"

Maxine Clark, Founder, Build-A-Bear Workshop

"I could recommend this book just on the basis of the interesting biographies of successful entrepreneurs, but the insights into the processes that made these visionaries successful is the real importance of the book. Lloyd's book codifies his keen business insights..."

James B. Cloonan, Chairman, American Association of Individual Investors

"A great collection of profiles of visionaries of our time, full of insights and captivating detail about leaders that changed our world."

Daniel Diermeier, Provost, The University of Chicago

"Shefsky's great story telling reveals new lessons on visionaries and their insights every aspiring leader should devour and embrace, particularly those seeking successional victory. This book speaks to the heart and America's heartland sustainable breakouts that make our capitalism so exceptional. It's so good I'm giving it to my son."

Ken Fisher, Founder and Executive Chairman, Fisher Investments and Four Time New York Times Bestselling Author.

"How to be a visionary? Imbibe the wisdom contained in this intriguing book of real life achievers. You'll also be inspired…."

Steve Forbes, Editor-in-Chief, President and CEO, Forbes

"Lloyd Shefsky has always offered readers, clients, and students the keys to entrepreneurial success. Here it is from the mouths of the moguls themselves, from the Wirtzes to the Perots, Kay Koplovitz to FedEx's Fred Smith. Shefsky gets behind the myths and the mystique and gets down to the invaluable nuts and bolts."

David Friend, Vanity Fair Creative Development Editor

"Lloyd Shefsky utilized a story telling technique to describe the challenges and ultimate success of a few handfuls of remarkable business leaders, many of which are long admired friends of mine. Leading... often takes a bumpy and lonely path requiring enormous work and tough-minded resilience....It is a quick and effective read."

Christopher Galvin, Former CEO, Motorola, Inc.; CEO and Co-Founder, Harrison Street Capital, LLC

"Lloyd Shefsky has done it again with his inspiring, superb story-telling. *Visionarie$ Are Made, Not Born* is the natural progression of his books on entrepreneurs and reinvention, with this twist: This one answers an age-old question. And nobody is better suited to answer that question than Lloyd, himself a visionary, who gained his unique perspective from a career built on getting up close and personal with some of the best visionaries of our time."

Herb Greenberg, Co-founder, Pacific Square Research; CNBC contributor; financial journalist

"Lloyd Shefsky provides an informative and interesting perspective on the 'vision thing.'
It is important for anyone interested in business."

Jack M. Greenberg, Former CEO, McDonald's

"Lloyd brings the reader inside the stories of a diverse and fascinating group of visionaries. Because he has not only studied the subject matter but knows these leaders,…he is able to bring to life themes and lessons…. There is much to be gained from reading this book."

Christie Hefner, Former Chairman, C.E.O., Playboy Enterprises, Inc.

"Once again, Lloyd has provided valuable lessons in leadership, not in theory, but with real world examples….This book should provide inspiration to anyone with initiative and an idea, of any kind and any size."

Stan Kasten, President & CEO, Los Angeles Dodgers; Former President of the Atlanta Braves, Hawks and Thrashers and the Washington Nationals.

"Visionaries are fascinating people who manage to develop a larger picture of possibility than their immediate peers. Read Lloyd's book and get inspired."

Philip Kotler, S.C.Johnson Distinguished Professor of International Marketing, Kellogg School of Management, Northwestern University.

"Business visionaries have always been defined in retrospect: 'You'll know it when you see it.' Shefsky provides a roadmap for seeing or becoming a visionary prospectively and proactively. What a valuable insight and tool!"

Larry Levy, Founder Levy Restaurants; Founder Diversified Real Estate Capital, LLC; Chairman, Del Taco

"Shefsky's *Visionarie$ are Made not Born* will make a good primer for all business visionaries and would-be business visionaries. He breaks the art of vision down into practical, manageable concepts that just about anybody can understand and offers up noteworthy examples to illustrate. Anyone interested in sharpening their vision-making skills should read this book."

Andrew Mills, President, Medline Industries, Inc.

"What if any of us could have founded Starbucks or Facebook? Lloyd Shefsky demystifies visionaries and makes their stories and approaches accessible to everyone. Read *Visionarie$ Are Made Not Born* if you're ready to make your mark on our world.

Mark Pincus, Founder & Executive Chairman, Zynga

"Upon reading Lloyd Shefsky's new book, *Visionarie$ Are Made Not Born*, I was impressed…that he, like few others, understands innovation and the motivations of visionary entrepreneurs with what seem to be impossible ideas….So, hold your hat, you will be surprised and motivated by his analysis of these remarkable people."

Hedy M Ratner, Founder and President Emerita, Women's Business Development Center

"Shefsky gets it! He pulls the cover off being a business visionary. *Visionarie$ Are Made Not Born* will show you the behavior you should learn and the results you should aim for. Whether you aspire to lead a big organization, a start-up or anything in between, you must read *Visionarie$ Are Made Not Born*. It will improve your perspective and approach."

John W. Rogers, Jr., Chairman, CEO & Chief Investment Officer, Ariel Investments, LLC.

"Lloyd's book should be required reading in our high schools, colleges and beyond….It is inspiring, honest and, most important, practical. Lloyd not only crystallizes the fundamental elements of vision, but also demonstrates how to make that vision a reality."

Joel B. Ronkin, Chief Executive Officer, Fekkai Brands and LUXE Brands

"In his book "*Visionarie$ Are Made Not Born,*" Lloyd Shefsky presents fascinating reports of interviews with men and women who have used their visions to create highly successful businesses. His discussion of the elements of those visions provides extremely useful advice for those seeking to create new enterprises or to improve established ones."

David Ruder, Former Chairman, Securities & Exchange Commission

"Yes, this is an inspiring business book, giving proof that America is still the land of great opportunity for those who dare to dream, and work hard. But ask yourself this question: What characteristics do these visionaries share that I could help instill in my children, grandchildren, and any child who crosses my path?"

Terry Savage, Nationally Syndicated Financial Columnist

"Once again, Shefsky displays his unique abilities…to bring us *Visionarie$ Are Made Not Born*, a must have book. I've used Lloyd's books in my classes with great success. This book has lessons for everyone."

Pramodita Sharma, Editor, Family Business Review; Sanders Professor of Family Business, University of Vermont

"Lloyd Shefsky has the great ability to enable visionaries to be comfortable in talking about themselves and what helped them become successful."

Murray L. Simpson, Former General Counsel, Franklin Templeton Investments

"Each chapter is an intriguing story in itself. This book will help bright people with a keen passion overcome obstacles to achieve outstanding success. I can vouch for some of the book's lessons based on my personal experiences as well as those of my Seattle neighbors at Amazon and Starbucks."

Jim Sinegal, Co-Founder, Director, and former CEO of Costco Wholesale

"Shefsky has done it again. In his third and most masterful book yet he's synthesized the collective wisdom of numerous successful visionaries from various walks of life to share insights gleaned from their experiences. Shefsky leverages his years of experience as a corporate attorney, business school professor and entrepreneur to provide keen and unique perspectives from his interview subjects....I continue to...benefit from the wisdom he imparts in *Visionarie$ Are Made Not Born*. I highly recommend it to those just starting out on their career journey as well as those who have already made it – its chock full of insightful wisdom."

Avi Steinlauf, CEO of Edmunds

"No one knows entrepreneurs better than Professor Lloyd Shefsky. In mining that experience he discovers that vision is the most misunderstood element of successful leadership and management philosophy. The stories, his very creative and paradigm-breaking thinking and insight are compelling."

John Ward, Clinical Professor & Co-Director Center for Family Enterprises, Kellogg School of Management

"Professor Shefsky is a world renowned expert on entrepreneurship. His new book brings unique new insights to the reader. His interviews with top visionaries, revealed through this terse presentation, familiarize the reader with Shefsky's latest findings and lessons.

This book is an excellent read for everyone involved with or interested in issues like vision, entrepreneurship and leadership. It is mind-broadening, as well as an excellent resource for future research."

Israel Zang, Former Vice-provost, Tel Aviv University; Professor Emeritus and former Dean, Coller (previously Recanati) School of Management, Tel Aviv University; and former president, Academic College of Tel Aviv Jaffa

VISIONARIE$

ARE MADE NOT BORN

Your Vision Can Lead to Breakthrough Success

BY LLOYD E. SHEFSKY

DOC/DOC

Print ISBN: 978-1-54391-049-0
eBook ISBN: 978-1-54391-050-6

Library of Congress Cataloging-in-Publication Data: 2017957384

Shefsky, Lloyd E.

Visionarie$ are made not born: how business icons leveraged 5 elements of vision and so can you /Lloyd E. Shefsky.
pages cm
ISBN (hardback): 978-1-54391-049-0

1. Business Vision. 2.Entrepreneurship. 3. New business enterprises—Management. 4. Small business—Management. 5. Family-owned business enterprises—Management.6. Business Visionaries. 7. Success in business. I. Title

Visionarie$ Are Made Not Born™ is a Trademark of Lloyd E. Shefsky Inc.

All quoted material is taken from interviews conducted by the author from 2014 through 2017 unless otherwise noted.

To communicate with the author, learn more about the book and the interviews, and be among the first to learn about new developments, Visit: www.lloydshefsky.com.

Also visit us on Facebook, LinkedIn and Twitter.

Dedicated to
My kids and grandkids,
who bring me joy and pride and who
expand and sharpen my perspective.

My dear wife, Natalie
who brings beauty, balance, good
sense and love to my life.

Table of Contents

WATCH THE INTERVIEWEES TELL THEIR STORIES FOLLOW THE LINKS SPECIAL OPPORTUNITY FOR YOU

See the note at the end of this book (preceding the Index), explaining how you can view the videos of my interviews where links (e.g., [Wirtz #1]) appear in the book.

Introduction

▼▼▼▼▼▼▼▼▼▼▼▼

In the movie, "Jobs," Steve Wozniak, gifted creator of the pioneering Apple 1 and Apple 2 personal computers, is miffed when he asks his co-founder and friend, Steve Jobs: *"What do you do? You can't write code, you're not an engineer, you're not a designer, you can't put a hammer to a nail. I built the circuit board; the graphical interface was stolen from Xerox Parc. Someone else designed the box. So how come, ten times in a day, I read 'Steve jobs is a genius'?"*

What did he do? The irascible Steve Jobs was considered one of the world's great visionaries. The New York Times obit said Jobs "led a cultural transformation in the way music, movies and mobile communications were experienced in the digital age." Apple was to become the world's most valuable equity by the time of Steve Jobs' untimely death at 56 in 2011.

Wozniak's dismay is understandable: After all, it would not have been unreasonable had someone said the true visionary of the iPhone was Chester Gould, the creator of Dick Tracy comic strips where, on January 13, 1946, he introduced a 2-way wrist radio. Besides Wozniak's unsurprising jealousy and focus on details (such as merely inventing the Apple computer), may indicate he was blinded by the bigger picture. Visionary magic seems achievable only by the gods—those whose vision has profound impact, ala Edison and Steve Jobs.

That makes the visionary a mystic, and the visionary's mysticism is elusive. This stems, however, from a lack of understanding. The many unappreciated visionaries—the mere mortal visionaries if you will—are unaware of their prospects but needn't be.

For most, the appraisal of visionaries is retrospective, a view formed after the visionary is proved successful. For those of us who must make earlier decisions, such as whether to assist or invest, the very concept of a "visionary" is daunting, even scary. Even a leader of an established company who proclaims a new vision (think: Bezos or Musk envisioning space exploration) may adversely affect the companies' stock prices. That may be attributable to perceived increased risk of the new venture and a digression from the stable venture, as much as the observers' inability to see the views as clearly as does the visionary.

A more realistic measure requires more knowledgeable assessors. And whatever the number of visionaries, their numbers could be expanded dramatically if business leaders had a better, more concrete understanding of the elements of vision: what it takes to be one and how to "learn" and "train" to be one.

The chapters in this book reveal nuances of a dozen superb business leaders I have interviewed about the role of vision in their work. My analysis will help you learn the elements of vision and will show you how to use them to cultivate your own vision in this, *Visionarie$ Are Made Not Born*.

Reducing Vision to its Elements

Visionaries are like Christopher Columbus. With his vision that the world was round, reaching India by sailing west seemed natural. He couldn't know he was right. But he had listened to tales of ancient mariners and believed there was land of some sort beyond the horizon.

Most sailors feared falling off the edge of the earth, much like those businesspeople who hug the shore and forego opportunity. Columbus sailed the uncharted waters.

He was a visionary who faced naysayers of every sort and at each hollow dawn when he was long at sea. Indeed, he was a business visionary, a true entrepreneur whose venture capital backer, Queen Isabella of Spain, took an inordinate financial share by today's standards.

But gaining royal favor was the Nobel Prize of its day. And like imaginative entrepreneurs of today, Columbus weighed anchor to the jeers of the "smart money." Yet he found treasure: a vast new world.

Like other great visionaries, Newton, Jefferson, Billy Mitchell, Einstein, Eisenhower and Herzl, Columbus won fame more than fortune. Corporate visionaries whose work brings fame? Not so many. Jobs, Gates, Bezos, Musk and a few of Silicon Valley's more recent super stars are famous exceptions. Patently, treasure is more common than visionary fame.

So what if you're not a magician or a Jobs, Gates, Bezos or Musk? Can you still be a business visionary?

To be a business visionary is not to be a sorcerer. The skill is neither heavenly nor mundane human talent. It is elegant, advanced human behavior, no more God-given than any other. It is achievable in degrees but needn't be the nth degree. Its value can prove extraordinary, financially and impact on people's lives, even when its scope is less than extraordinary. In other words, one needn't be a superhero to be a business visionary, but that doesn't negate their special stature and skills.

Visionaries' visions are not bound by the restrictions of optics. It is not the product of eyes looking forward and certainly not bending periscope-like around walls and impediments. Nor is the object of such vision tangible or even familiar.

The visionaries' visions are figments of their imaginations, residing in their minds. It is not a sighting. One needn't travel to the future and return with a picture of what will be. Rather one devises thoughts as to what the future could be.

There is rarely a straight line to a vision. The shortest distance between a visionary and his or her vision is a function of strategies, tactics and skills of implementation by self or in collaboration with others.

A few years ago I told a reporter, Mildred Culp, "You don't have to see around corners. Seeing the writing on the walls of the box that contains you enables you to see and think out of that box." Since then, that view has become complicated with a new paradox I've noticed: Visions are often nearer than ever, yet more difficult. Sure, the likes of Bezos and Musk may envision outer space, (Bezos recently said his vision is to have millions of humans living and working in outer space by 2020), but for many, their business vision is as near as their closest competitor and as proximate as the next quarter. So what's so difficult? The difficulty was obvious when it entailed seeing far out, but now it's not so far out.

Today, the trick is seeing the vision faster not necessarily further. Change and innovation move quantum leaps faster in so many areas that vision must be immediately followed by planning and implementation, lest competitors or even the vision itself may bypass the visionary.

That is not to imply that the road to one's vision is uncluttered and devoid of barriers. Indeed, there are always impediments—in the present, the future, and even from the past. I refer to those as "vision collisions."

Visionaries and their visions are likely to confront the barriers, some seemingly impenetrable walls, others minor bumps in the road. Successful visionaries must overcome the walls and bumps, to avoid the collisions, sometimes doable with minor pivots. Other times there are forces or things that collide with the vision. The vision may be so powerful as to survive the collision and continue on its merry way. Or it may be necessary to have a new or updated vision, and that process may repeat itself over and over.

A vision's collision may be with a company culture gone awry, as was the case with Keith Williams, the CEO of Underwriter Laboratories. Or the clash may be with societal cultures, as it was for Kay Koplovitz and Fred Smith.

In family businesses the vision of the successor may collide with that of the predecessor, as occurred in the Perot, Wirtz, Terlato and Bigelow families. Handled properly, the successor's vision is merely the baton in a relay race, where the predecessor's smooth handoff leads to success and a collision between two runners would be catastrophic.

For companies whose sights are focused on the bottom line, the collisions may be between value and values, as it was for Rick Waddell of Northern trust.

As technologies develop at ever-increasing paces, "the way it's always been done," because that was the best way it could be done, confronts new overpowering technology enabling new visions, as it did for Robert Walter at Cardinal Health, David Abney at UPS, Fred Smith at Federal Express, and even at the goliath, IBM.

My analysis is grounded in a few dimensions. First, a premise: It is not a prerequisite that a visionary's vision must be to change the world or even a substantial part of it. One can qualify as a visionary by having a vision to change a company, a relatively limited market, and a relatively small number of people's lives.

Second I focus on the elements of vision. How do visionaries see what they see? What is the scope of their creativity in that foresight? How did they perceive, measure, define and limit the nature of problems that lead to needing a vision to solve those problems? Sometimes, visions derive from sighting opportunities not problems, and often it is a mixture of the two.

I do not believe that business visions derive from a commercial big bang. Rather, some actually search for a vision, expanding or tapering it as they discover, uncover or create technology or other means to make their vision feasible.

Third, I examine vision collision, the process by which a vision bumps into or is bumped by other forces: long-standing cultures or customs; solid or misguided beliefs; established power, dominance and intransigence; predecessors' focuses and preferences; customers' needs, demands or lack of knowledge; internal compasses regarding right and wrong; paradoxes between value and values; etc.

My book limns a dozen visionaries, some little known outside the trade and a few quite famous but little understood. I tell how they succeeded in spectacular ways.

More important, I'll show you the way to have visions like these corporate masters did by revealing their methods.

Vision and thus visionaries are too broad and amorphous to group let alone emulate. Therefore, I break down vision to its essential components or elements, arbitrary perhaps, but helpful to visionary aspirants. I call the elements, Beyond- the-Eaves Vision, Forest & Trees Vision, Trend Pattern Vision, Rapid Action Vision and finally Retro Vision.

Let's start with Beyond-the-Eaves Vision.

Five Elements of Vision

▼▼▼▼▼▼▼▼▼▼▼▼

1) Beyond-The-Eaves Vision

Columbus had never seen India and certainly didn't have one of those magnificent photos of Earth taken by our astronauts. His vision lacked direct visuals, being based on his observations and those of others. He listened to the tales of the ancient mariners, he watched ships' masts slip - not fall - off the horizon as he sailed, and he was rational about this. He demonstrated what I call Beyond-the-Eaves Vision. A Beyond-the-Eaves business visionary weighs the meaning of the wider horizons he sees.

This business person sees what others are doing in their businesses. This skill is requisite to discovering techniques and trends that may be applied to one's own business. Then one needs to become adept at copying others' ideas and visions.

Columbus's views extended only to the horizon because he lacked the means for extended vision. However, his vision wasn't inhibited by walls and protective lawyers. His vision was necessarily developed despite a lack of role models, a helpful barrier to others' entry as competitors. Columbus's observations lacked precision. Yet, in Columbus's mind, the vision of a globally-shaped Earth was so clear that he willingly risked lives, his own along with those of his terrified crew, and he convinced a queen to back him. His venture had a plank that puts TV's "Shark Tank" to shame.

Such commitment comes only when visions assume the clarity and certainty of reality. Today's business leaders have access to facts, photos and familiarity. *Columbus's vision derived from tales, optics and imagination. Both were and are obtained by looking at occurrences beyond one's lot line, which in real estate terms helps define property borders.*

2) Forest & Trees Vision

World War II is and hopefully will remain the largest war in history. Its battles were not limited to fighting fields. There were constant clashes among the Allies' political and military leaders: between those who pushed for the big picture and others who focused on details. There were great leaders in each perspective camp, not so many in both. Most had to choose: the forest or the trees, the big picture or the smaller detailed picture.

Gen. Dwight (Ike) Eisenhower seemed possessed of both. He could debate details with Gen. Patten and politics with Roosevelt and Churchill. It was the uncanny ability to see both the forest and the trees simultaneously that enabled him to manage the greatest invasion in history and bring victory over the enemy.

The successful business visionary must be able to distinguish the global aspects of the company and its industry, the forest, from the company's people, financial situation, capabilities and local challenges, the trees that constitute the forest. Business visionaries do so by alternating between the two instantly and automatically.

Such visionaries have the ability to focus virtually simultaneously on the smallest company trees and the whole world forest including the competition, the economies (global and local) and relevant time frames.

3) Trend Pattern Vision

Price, quality and service are the three-legged stool of business. They begin in sync. Advancing one of these is often the basis for competitive advantage. Observing the pace of trends in all or any of the three is an example of the Trending Pattern Vision that serves as the base for many business successes.

When inefficiencies caused a few airlines to raise fares, reduce services and eliminate the fun factor in air travel, others with Beyond-the-Eaves

Vision saw it as a license to do the same. One airline leader's vision clashed with the entire industry.

Herb Kelleher was co-founder of Southwest Airlines. He saw those trends and envisioned opportunity. From out of nowhere Southwest soared to the third largest US carrier. This was the result of Herb's looking beyond the wing span and seeing trends in competitors' actions and customers' desires. He allowed flight attendants and pilots to use the public address system to entertain passengers. This and efficiency-enhancing measures made flying a pleasurable experience and not the boring bus ride his rivals were providing.

Spotting a trend is a great skill but nowhere near as valuable as being able to follow its path and the speed at which it is moving. Business visionaries who can spot such trend patterns and convince others to follow their lead have more time to reposition their companies to take advantage of opportunities the trends offer, to avoid pitfalls trends cause, and to prevent wasting resources chasing lost causes.

4) Rapid Action Vision

For most business leaders, visions develop over time. But one dare not take too long. Visionaries win the gold. Silver winners? Forgotten or remembered for failure. Most business visionaries are lucky to have one vision that carries their company to success; some have a series of lesser but equally important visions that, taken together, rank in importance with the other visions.

Such rapid repetitive visions present themselves most frequently in areas of intense time pressure: combat, medical crises, natural and terrorist disasters, criminal and fire emergencies, and competitive sports. In those, a form of response differentiates winners and losers.

Some refer to a rapid recognition from experiences as a sixth sense. Similar traits are present in certain business visionaries. Rapidity is relative. In war, rapid may be in seconds, while in business, rapid may mean months or even years, since the business visionary usually experiences such change in decades. Few have such a series, each with grand visions.

One who has is Jeff Bezos, founder and CEO of Amazon. Today, it's difficult to analyze the pieces of Amazon. It is truly an amalgam of Jeff Bezos's Rapid Action Visions. Starting with books, he recognized the inefficiencies of an antiquated industry, run essentially by English majors. Then, having built a customer base, he expanded into other products, then further, built an extraordinary system for marketing and logistics, a platform for others to sell products, and for others to store things in Amazon's cloud: more recently, buying airplanes to reduce dependence on UPS, Fed Ex and the USPS, while continuing development and acceptance of bantam delivery drones to fill his latest vision.

Each of his visions requires successful implementation utilizing the previous visions as the infrastructure and launch pad for the newer ones. Some resulted from thought processes that also visualized a completed prior vision even before proven or existent. Yet the prior vision was so real in his mind that its projection provided ample infrastructure for the next.

5) Retro Vision

A new vision can call for the rebirth of an old vision for re-use. The visionary recognizes that the values and standards of the past constitute infrastructure that can be applied in the present to lay new roads for the future.

This vision occurs infrequently, less often than it should, possibly because: (i) we are admonished from childhood not to look back, not to dwell on past results, and only to focus on future challenges and opportunities; and (ii) looking back may necessitate looking too far back to be meaningful. (However, Sir Winston Churchill said, "The farther backward you can look, the farther forward you are likely to see.")

Time lapse is a challenge to all visions, so looking far back can be difficult. But Retro Vision is a growing technique among family businesses. S. C. Johnson is but one of millions of family businesses. Originally known as Johnson Wax, the enterprise has diversified and modernized. Successful now in several industries and best known for products such as Raid, Pledge, Off, Glade, Drano, Windex and Ziploc, S. C. Johnson has grown in volume, *locations and number of employees into a highly successful and competitive 21st-century enterprise.*

The future is theirs. Yet over the past couple of decades, they have purposefully reached back to their roots, finding the origin of their values that provided the basis for extraordinary success.

They even started tagging all their TV and print ads with, "a family business." Peering back decades, even generations, their extraordinary Retro Vision provided the infrastructure and guard rails for moving forward.

THE VISION THING

Visionarie$ Are Made Not Born

The title of my first book, *Entrepreneurs Are Made Not Born*, was selected by my extremely capable editor, Caroline Carney, who spotted the phrase in my text and elevated it to a title. A similar question—genetic or environmental—reappears regarding business visionaries. That's not obvious. Not all business visionaries are entrepreneurs, although one might claim that all entrepreneurs are business visionaries.

Business visionaries certainly have both genetic and environmental influences. I don't pretend to have the magic recipe for those ingredients. Since I doubt that anyone does, I suggest: It's too late to choose your parents, so focus on what you can affect.

The Nearsighted Critic

In *Invent Reinvent Thrive*, I used a saying I created over 40 years ago: "If you're not up on it, then you have to be down on it," to explain that many naysayers are such because they don't understand another's idea. Applying that to business visionaries, I would use the optics analogy: The visionary is far-sighted, seeing things further away (in distance or time) that aren't visible to others who, in effect, are nearsighted.

CHAPTER 1

Rocky Wirtz

The Chicago Blackhawks' Story
Rocky Inherited a Team of Lukewarm
Losers Plus Chilling Debt: Could His Vision
Make the Blackhawks Hot on Ice Again?

▼▼▼▼▼▼▼▼▼▼▼▼▼

*R*ocky Wirtz and his grandfather, Arthur Wirtz, lived in totally different worlds, and each needed different leadership techniques to lead the family's best-known business, the Chicago Blackhawks. For Arthur, the Great Depression enabled him to snap up the Chicago Stadium for pennies on the dollar. As savvy realtor turned impresario, Arthur brought the city a star-studded hockey team and other iconic stars of the day: famed skater Sonia Henie and movie cowboys like Roy Rogers who settled for modest pay in that desperate era. When Arthur died, his son, Bill, a CPA/bean counter, focused on Arthur's tightfisted approach to talent after the super pay era in sports arrived. Arthur had lost hockey super star Bobby Hull who skated back to Canada, a million dollar contract in hand. In time there were nearly as many players as fans at the stadium. Under CEO Bill, the Blackhawks remained a poorly run hobby. The family thrived with solid well-run real estate, banking and spirits businesses. Bill's son, Rocky, grew up in the lap of luxury, which generally leads to low expectations. Rocky disproved the "silver spoon syndrome." He worked in sales in the spirit business,* *where he developed business vision and techniques. On Bill's death Rocky, took over the Blackhawks: saw crushing sums were due the team. In hockey, the blue line initiates a change of direction. In the Wirtz family, the critical line was not on the ice but in the P&L statements. Where Arthur and Bill focused "below the line" (on reducing expenses), Rocky's vision was to change the focus to "above the line" (increasing revenue). Sensing potential, he spent heavily to win games and inspire fans, ultimately increasing team values beyond his wildest dreams. Rocky's vision led to breakaway success.*

Rocky Wins Back Fans and the Coveted Cup

It was a sight to behold: the Stanley Cup trophy—hoisted high, in celebration of the Blackhawks having won the 2010 Championship of the National Hockey League.

The Cup is nearly 3 feet high and weighs almost 35 pounds. Its silver gleamed in reflection of the bright lights of the stadium and it symbolized a team that had risen to the top in just a few years in the wake of five decades without signal success.

It reflected on a team that had played harder and better than any other. It reflected on the fans who returned to the Stadium to celebrate and to adore the team they had cheered to victory.

But most interestingly, it reflected on the man who was holding the trophy high above his head, his face gleaming like the silver trophy itself.

That man was Rocky Wirtz, CEO of the Chicago Blackhawks. Like any sports team owner, though never personally involved in the slugfests that animated the games, he was entitled to celebrate along with the players who had fought so valiantly on the ice. It seemed natural and deserved. In fact it was anything but natural, and he deserved monumental credit.

Arthur Wirtz: Frugal Titan with a Flair for Showmanship

By the beginning of the Great Depression, Chicago businessman Arthur Wirtz had amassed a safe fortune in his home town consisting of secure rental properties—a real estate portfolio without attendant debt—an enviable position when the Great Depression hit and wiped out many of his peers who were saddled with massive debt that led to bankruptcies.

Then Arthur acted out of form. He bought the Chicago Stadium. Even to the penny-pinching Arthur Wirtz the property was irresistibly priced at just pennies on the dollar. Yet while it was a high visibility, trophy property, Wirtz was fully aware that it was valuable only if it generated revenue and profits.

To that end and acting out of character – or so it had seemed then— Arthur Wirtz became an impresario. He created ice shows and recruited the Olympic Gold Medal winner Sonja Henie to bring her sparkle to the Stadium ice and brought in cowboy movie stars such as Roy Rogers, Gene Autry and Hopalong Cassidy.

He gained controlling interest in a West Coast hockey team and brought it to Chicago. It promptly became the city's beloved Blackhawks Hockey Team. With few teams in the NHL and Depression era wages, top players were inexpensive, and Arthur could build a successful team with an enviable record that filled the seats and brought immediate profits.

Arthur's various business interests: real estate, banking, hockey and most profitable of all importation and distribution of spirits did spectacularly well during his era. He created an immense personal net worth. This gave him hefty power in the city of Chicago—and well beyond its borders. Of this, make no mistake: Arthur was a tough businessman. There was never a question as to who was boss. Arthur ran the enterprise according to his ideas only, most of them sound, but a few, whimsical at best.

It's My Stick and My Puck, So It's My Way or The Highway

When Arthur Wirtz died in 1983, the mantel fell to his son, Bill, an accountant who gave up a budding career to return to the family enterprise. He thrived at his father's side. Thus, when Arthur passed away, succession was seamless: for father and son had developed a virtually identical mind set. Both operated the non-sports businesses aggressively, employing traditional management techniques: though some said a bit more intensely than competitors.

But when it came to the Blackhawks, their shared mind set exposed a totally different vision reflecting anything but traditional management techniques. A bean counting style sent a clear message to Blackhawk staff: Arthur and son Bill considered the team their private hobby.

The message to the fans was worse. The Wirtz dictate: home games were not to be aired on TV. After all, they said, who would pay to see a game that you could see for free at home? Maybe that wasn't so bad for the fans, considering the quality of the roster. The Hawks ceased fielding top talent when stars demanded fatter salaries. When Blackhawk super star, Bobby Hull, threatened to move to Canada for a million dollar package, Bill approved Arthur's decision not to match the offer. He echoed his Dad's dictum: Do not waste a fortune on players. When Bobby Hull left, the fans never forgave the two.

You might say the two men ran the Blackhawks with a *Field of Dreams* outlook: "build it and they will come."

That was, of course, the catchphrase from that wonderful movie about baseball. It almost never works in real life.

Indeed, in Chicago, it was read as a type of arrogance, sounding like the fans should be thankful to Arthur and Bill Wirtz for allowing the team to exist in their beloved city.

Actually, it wasn't all arrogance. When Arthur became an impresario in the Depression era, he met the salary demands of the big stars as those costs were modest by today's standards.

But when the Depression ended and world famed skater Sonja Henie demanded more, Arthur replaced Sonja with Barbara Ann Scott, the successor Olympic skating champ. He willingly fielded less-known talent to save money.

That's because Arthur was first and foremost a financial guy and son, Bill, was, yes, an accountant. Between the two, there was a clear focus below the line, on expense items. Their way to improving business results - at least at the Blackhawks - was by cutting costs.

They were less attuned to marketing and promoting the hockey team. Their marketing was focused on preventing anyone from taking advantage of them. That's what led to their policy of not allowing home games to appear on TV.

Rocky Wirtz: Liquor Maven Inherits a Goal-less Hockey Team

Rocky grew up in and among the family enterprises. Just out of college, he heard Arthur and Bill discussing their unique entre into multistate distribution of liquor, a new concept which had yet to be adopted by most in the industry. This was a rocky road if you will. Each state had its own laws regarding liquor distribution. Exclusionary state laws had kept the distribution business divided by state, precluding efficiencies of volume while retaining organizational and bureaucratic burdens. Rocky was excited by the profit prospects of breaking new ground.

True, Rocky was a hockey fan. He had attended games since the age of eight. But the liquor business intrigued him the most—especially the marketing and sales aspects. His hockey involvement was to show up for the annual team picture and to go to occasional league meetings as an Alternative Governor.

When Rocky's brother, Peter, became active with the Blackhawks, Rocky's involvement tapered to nil. Peter had no interest in the other businesses. He and the boys' dad, Bill, worked closely on Blackhawk matters and Rocky was "walled off."

As Rocky put it, "We'd have a meeting, and they'd start talking hockey. You'd realize that you really weren't welcome, so you'd just get up and excuse yourself. It felt funny: it's like watching a train wreck. You can't control it, even though you know it's going to happen."

Explaining his non-role to me, Rocky added: "From that standpoint, it was disconcerting, but I had other things to do." [Wirtz #1]

There were times when Rocky tried to express his opinions, effectively contradicting those of his father and brother. He told them outright—and fruitlessly—that he disagreed with them regarding their refusal to televise games.

And there was an incident regarding the team physician. They had a good team doctor, a Dr. Terry, but agreed to a change in order to secure a $100,000 sponsorship from the University of Chicago Hospitals.

Rocky found this ludicrous. Dr. Terry was after all a hockey specialist. "You are risking the players' futures. Why don't you just get your sales force to go out and raise $100,000 instead?"

These vision collisions seemed too much. Despite the fact that Bill was extraordinarily caring, even paternalistic, toward his players, Rocky's remark got a look from his dad and his brother that suggested he had three heads. Peter wasn't an accountant, but he always did what he thought his father wanted rather than what *he* actually wanted to do. Together, they couldn't get past their financial orientation of cutting expenses and letting sales take care of themselves."

Rocky went on to say the two never accepted his recommendations with regard to marketing and/or sales.

It wasn't only Rocky who was rejected: "Everyone was scared to talk. It was like the 'Emperor's Clothes.' No one wanted to tell the emperor he didn't have any clothes on."

That inhibited any sales effort. "We had these holes, and no one could do anything to fill them. No one had the authority to do anything. No one was listening to the customers."

▼▼▼▼▼▼▼▼▼▼▼▼▼▼▼▼▼▼▼▼▼▼▼▼▼▼▼▼▼

Cumulative Losses Add Up to a Gain

All businesses may seem alike, but sports teams are businesses like no other. They are structured and run to earn little or no current income, because they invest in expensive players and venues, to attract fans in person and as TV viewers.

Fans in the stadium not only buy tickets at prices that can increase as teams' quality and results improve, but also spend on concessions, parking and souvenirs.

Indeed, quality players can even generate royalties for paraphernalia with team and player identification, purchased elsewhere, pretty much 24/7. And as TV viewership increases, ever more lucrative contracts with broadcasters can lead to huge revenues.

The business of sports compels spending each year's increased cash flow and generally even more, to create a continuous cycle of growing revenue, even though the increased spending perpetuates operating losses.

Why, you may ask, would anyone perpetuate operating losses? By achieving continuous growth, the value of the enterprises increases, in amounts far-exceeding the aggregate operating losses.

In addition, the higher valuation, in the event of a sale of the team, is taxed at far more favorable capital gains tax rates. Those principles guide the mind frame of sports team owners.

The Blackhawks, under Arthur and Bill, ignored those Principles. After all, they'd never sell the team. It was their hobby, not their "real business." So why consider such principles?

Their commitment to cost cutting, resulted in a poorer product, antagonized fans, and brought forth a slide in rather than an improvement in the Blackhawks team value.

"What he did," Rocky said of his father, "was, to use a hockey term—put me in the penalty box. This took "checking," the hockey term for colliding with another player, into the physical realm of vision collision. During that time, he would talk to me about business but would not discuss anything personal. In the two years when he didn't talk to me personally, I didn't come to Thanksgiving dinner and didn't have anything to do with Christmas.

"He said, 'I'll deliver your present,' and I said, 'That's fine.'" Rocky's father felt he could manage the hockey business without his son the liquor specialist and he chose not to listen to him or anyone else who said the emperor was naked.

But Rocky knew that his dad needed the liquor business relationships that Rocky had created so successfully.

"As he was getting older he couldn't have the same kind of relationships as I did, so he had to deal with me. I knew that in my arena [the spirits business] I could make things work. I'd always make it his idea and would generally get what I wanted to get done. I just had to make sure that by the end of the conversation, he was convinced that it was his idea."

▼▼▼▼▼▼▼▼▼▼▼▼▼▼▼▼▼▼▼▼▼▼▼▼▼▼▼▼

Rocky's Grandfather's Family Vision: What Did Arthur See?

Holiday boycotts by Bill, marketing extortion by Rocky—and you thought playing hockey was a tough sport! What a bizarre situation, especially among natural allies in one family.

One might assume, given the relationship between Peter and Bill, Peter would be chosen to run the Blackhawks organization when Bill died. And had it been up to Bill, that might have happened, with heaven knows what result.

Oddly, however, the late Arthur Wirtz had provided in his will and trusts that Rocky was to run the family enterprise, including the team, after Bill was gone. It seems the entrepreneur, realtor and impresario was also clairvoyant.

▲▲▲▲▲▲▲▲▲▲▲▲▲▲▲▲▲▲▲▲▲▲▲▲▲▲▲▲

When I said to Rocky that his grandfather had tried to control from the grave, he said he had never discussed that with his dad. Rocky said, "Everyone knew that dad had to control everything, but it was a real problem for me that he couldn't accept anything he couldn't control. Everyone knew that I was going to be running these businesses, because that's how my grandfather set it up. So instead of fighting it, dad should have made it easier. But dad couldn't accept the fact that he was still being controlled by his dad, my grandfather. So I had to wait for dad to die before I could learn what to do."

Bill Passes On, and a Bill is Presented

Losing your dad is always difficult, but in 2007, during the week after Bill's death, Rocky's life was in turmoil. He had assumed the position of CEO of the enterprise and sent a clear message as to who was in charge by cleaning out Arthur's office and moving in. His grandfather's office hadn't been used by anybody in over two decades.

As that was happening, Rocky received a memo that the Blackhawks had run out of money. In effect, they presented Rocky with a bill for $40 million to cover the players' payroll. The new CEO had no idea things were that bad. It was bizarre: [Wirtz #2]

"I walked into the Blackhawk's office, about 3 or 4 days after Dad's passing. I noticed people weren't talking to each other. They stayed in their offices. There was no idle chitchat, no passive communication, nothing at all.

"At first, I thought it was because dad had passed away and that people might be frightened about the future. But I realized that they were completely at odds with what to do or with doing anything. There was no camaraderie even, nothing.

"I said that I wanted to get some bottled water to take back to the office. They told me there was a five-gallon jug and plastic beer glasses in the kitchen. I could fill a glass and take it back to the desk. It turned out the same was true in the locker room. Those large Hinckley Springs jugs were available but no small bottles because Peter had thought it was too expensive. [Wirtz #3]

"No sum was too small to save, not even a nickel. The idea culture was to save our way into prosperity. I didn't agree with that. I had spent 30 plus years on the sales side of the business.

"Driving sales was my orientation. Through the years, I'd asked them if they wanted to cross promote. We had some very good sales executives in the liquor business, but they wanted nothing to do with any of those individuals. It was not a selling culture. We clearly needed to develop one quickly."

By this time Peter had sent a letter telling Rocky that he did not want to be involved with the Blackhawks. He was going to concentrate on his side of the business: concession vending.

This was in September of 2007, and the nation was entering its worst financial crisis since the depression. The banks were in serious trouble. Rocky says he was baffled: "We had a lot of bank stocks, and banks were stopping their dividends. For practical purposes, I didn't know how much cash I would need: I knew how much I would need for the Blackhawks, but not how much of an income stream there would be. Scary times, and we needed to preserve capital."

Did it make sense to pour water into a melting ice rink? The most basic issues at Blackhawk offices went un-served.

Rocky discovered in his first days at the Blackhawk offices that there was no one there to answer the phones. This was left to college interns who didn't come in every day. Phones rang incessantly. Rocky was exasperated: "Salesmen can't stand the sound of unanswered phones."

Rocky was a highly-effective salesman; the Blackhawks jangling phones drove him crazy. He realized this was part of a bigger problem.

"None of the sales people would make telephone calls. That's because they realized the first thing out of a customer's mouth was 'Why aren't you putting home games on TV?'

"They didn't have an answer to it. So they stayed in their offices. The last place you want your salesmen is in the office. You want them in the customers' offices, where the customers feel comfortable—where they think they have a leg up on you.

"Fundamentally, in talking to people in the office, they actually believed that the Wirtz family thought hockey didn't need to make money because hockey was just a hobby.

"I don't mind a hobby for $100,000, but I can't have a $40 million hobby. Yet this permeated the atmosphere of the office. [Wirtz #4]

"We, being the Blackhawks, had burned every bridge to all of our customers and all of our fans. Your sponsor is also your customer. So is the press and so are your players. You need all those relationships. Yet for whatever reasons, those relationships for the Blackhawks were very poor."

▼▼▼▼▼▼▼▼▼▼▼▼▼▼▼▼▼▼▼▼▼▼▼▼▼▼▼▼▼▼▼▼▼▼▼▼

Inherited Vision But Different Strategies and Tactics

When Bill died, the Blackhawks were valued at about $120 million. Of course that's a hypothetical valuation by the media; there was no guarantee that they'd receive that much in a sale.

Still, that may sound like a lot of money. But it's actually quite low as far as sports team valuations go. Beyond-the-Eaves Vision revealed to Rocky how valuable other teams had become, and Trend Pattern Vision projected even better days ahead. Forest & Trees Vision indicated that he could build the Blackhawks to take advantage of such prospects.

Besides, the Blackhawks value at the current level was a small fraction of the overall value of the Wirtz enterprises.

To many that would seem a good time to bail out, to sell the team and invest the proceeds in the family's more profitable businesses. Of course, that philosophy would've been similar to that of Arthur's naysayers—who probably told Arthur not to invest in the stadium, or later, in the Blackhawks but instead to invest in the family's real estate business.

Here, Arthur and Rocky had similar ambitious visions. They differed on other business decisions, such as operational tactics, but ultimately, the visions are more important.

Today, the Blackhawks' value in the marketplace would be closer to $1 billion than to the $120 million that might have been realized in a 2007 sale of the team.

▲▲▲▲▲▲▲▲▲▲▲▲▲▲▲▲▲▲▲▲▲▲▲▲▲▲▲▲▲▲▲▲▲▲▲▲

Forest & Trees Vision enabled Rocky to see the real assets of the Blackhawks, even as he contemplated paying its huge bills. He saw the solution to the balance sheet could be found in a new way of visualizing the P&L statement, focusing above not below the line–focusing on revenue growth not cost savings.

Rocky decided he should start with getting games on TV. So, Rocky made an appointment to visit with the Comcast people.

As was his style, Rocky showed up on time. "They were shocked that we started the meeting on time. To me it was just showing respect for other peoples' time. I try to be punctual, especially so if it is a business engagement that is at stake. Here it set the tone: showed them we're going to run this as a business.

"The Comcast personnel felt they could not sell TV time for Blackhawk games because it was late in the season [after advertisers' budgets would have been committed elsewhere] and because advertisers had lost interest in the Blackhawks."

In answer to Rocky's inquiry, Comcast said it would have charged $500 for a 30 second ad spot but would probably be lucky to get $400. Still they felt they couldn't sell advertisers on buying Blackhawk spots.

Comcast estimated that the cost of putting select games on TV would approximate $450,000. Comcast refused to risk this; they wanted money in hand. Being in the spirits business, Rocky was well aware of the old saying, "Talk is cheap; it takes money to buy whiskey."

TV advertising is a very structured, seasonal business. Budgets for the ensuing year and allocations to different shows or even different media often start two years in advance with commitment decisions made up to a year in advance.

Coming in after the season had started resulted in an uphill climb for Rocky. The slope of that climb was exacerbated by the Blackhawks' terrible performance, its lack of a meaningful audience, and a general lack of confidence in the Blackhawk's organization. It was, therefore, impossible for Rocky to sell Comcast on the Blackhawks. He sold Comcast, instead, on his own reading of the situation. And he couldn't do that with mere words. He demonstrated his vision with his deeds.

The two sides were at a stalemate. Rocky knew he had to bear the burden of proof. He had to demonstrate that he would be proactive, that he would make things happen. So he said he would cover the cost. Gutsy.

Then he went to companies with whom the other Wirtz businesses had good relationships. He went to Diageo, the huge spirits bottler, where he "told a little white lie," saying that the phones were ringing off the hook with people wanting the TV spots. He said most of the spots already had sponsors, and that this was one of the few spots left. Diageo bought the hundred thousand dollars spot.

In Hollywood, agents will manage to sign a star by saying they have already signed another star the first star greatly admires. Then they defuse their white lie by honestly telling the second star they have the first star under contract.

Rocky did the same with the Chicago Chevy Dealers and others. It worked. At long last, Blackhawk games would be on TV, just a few times in that first partial year but later, all games. [Wirtz #5]

There was more work to be done. Rocky needed coverage: "The newspapers were not following the Blackhawks. We found they'd cut travel budgets: Didn't even let reporters accompany the Blackhawks to Detroit for an away game."

One other thing: attendance at the Stadium was abysmal. "I knew I had to get to the newspapers," Rocky said, "so I went to the Tribune, Sun Times and the Daily Herald. I'll never forget, I went to the Daily Herald on a Friday afternoon. They didn't expect us to be working as the weekend approached.

"I walked in, and it was like the old E.F. Hutton TV commercial: 'When E. F. Hutton Talks: People listen.' They all stopped as I walked by their desks." They stared at Rocky looking at him like he was some kind of freak: "I gave them my card and introduced myself. I said I was working on the Hawks and I'd appreciate it if they could review their travel budgets, because it was important for people to read about the Hawks.

"I think they were surprised because in the past, they would be summoned to the United Center (that replaced The Chicago Stadium in 1994), to the Sonja Henie Room, where Dad held court. Press people were required to come for lunch." [Wirtz #6]

What a come down. Not only had Blackhawks ticket sales fallen to 3,400 per game but the United Center stadium could accommodate more than 10 times that number. Players got tickets to pass on to friends, inviting them to attend free.

How ironic! Here was a system that wouldn't give free TV to fans, out of fear that they would not attend the games, yet gave them free tickets to attend the games. It made no sense.

Rocky thought long and hard. He had to determine the best approach for dealing with the problem. Clearly the status quo was untenable. He had to do something new, something creative, something constructive, but most of all he had to exhibit a very different attitude and get customers to buy into his vision for the Blackhawks' future if anything was to work.

Not Every Losing Manager Makes Money for His Team

Rocky had heard of John McDonough, the President of the Chicago Cubs organization. McDonough had a very impressive record with the Cubs organization. He filled the seats and made money despite the Cubs' notoriously terrible playing record.

As Hall of Fame broadcaster, Jack Brickhouse, said of the Cubs he'd long covered play by play, "Any team can have a bad century." The Cubs hadn't won a world series since 1908. (In a result accepted with near riotous enthusiasm by millions of fans, the Chicago Cubs finally won the World Series in 2016. To borrow a cold remedy ad phrase: "Oh, what a relief it is.")

Beyond-the-Eaves Vision convinced Rocky that McDonough was his man. But the two had never met. He tried to arrange for a meeting through an intermediary. McDonough indicated he was about to leave town for several weeks. Rocky called him back and told him he couldn't wait a month and needed to talk to him right away.

They wound up meeting on a Saturday, in the Western suburbs, by no means convenient to Rocky's office or home. Scheduled for less than an hour, the meeting went on for hours. No command performance in the Sonja Henie Room for Rocky. Who says the apple doesn't fall far from the tree?

Rocky told John that he was not talking to anyone who didn't already have a job. He was only talking to people who did have jobs. Rocky knew that in 20 years with the Cubs, John had never won anything. His secret weapon: Rocky explaining that he was going to build a team that could win the Stanley Cup.

He also told John he didn't know what he was earning at the Cubs but he would not pay him more: "This is not a move to see how much money you can make. It's to see whether you want to come do something exciting with me." Rocky was a great salesman and he closed the sale. John took the job. [Wirtz #7]

Loyalty with a Caveat

The Wirtz family was very loyal to its people, but there is a point where the loyalty has to stop. As Rocky put it to me:

"You must put the company first: which comes first, the chicken or the egg? The chicken. It can produce more eggs."

Day to day the Blackhawks were managed by Bob Pulford, a former Canadian hockey player who was loved by the Wirtz family and the team. But he had wanted to retire for years.

"I learned a long time ago that when someone has retired mentally, you're not doing him or the company any good keeping him. But Dad kept bringing him back. I couldn't fire Pully but he might interfere with what McDonough had to do."

Instead of letting him go, Rocky moved him to the corporate office, together with Pully's assistant. And Rocky made him an Alternate Governor to the NHL. These and other changes went well with most family members but not with Rocky's siblings. [Wirtz #8]

They felt Rocky was being disloyal to their father: "No, I'm not being disloyal. I've been trained always to put the company first. I'm not being disloyal to Dad; I just don't agree with him." [Wirtz #9]

Rocky never was able to change his sibling's frame of mind, even though the wisdom of his decisions should have become evident as his efforts succeeded in spectacular fashion.

"My stepmother would select the music the organist played during the Blackhawk home games. This was like going to a mortuary. This was the most boring music I ever heard." Rocky changed that and he also talked to people at the games. [Wirtz #10]

▼▼▼▼▼▼▼▼▼▼▼▼▼▼▼▼▼▼▼▼▼▼▼▼▼▼▼▼▼▼▼▼

The Unclothed Emperor Had All the Trappings of a Castle

Rocky's reference to his father "holding court" can't be taken lightly. Bill had the persona, as well as the trappings to go with a royal court in the stadium itself. He had the Sonja Henie Room. He had secure seating for himself and other important people, highly visible but inaccessible to Hawks fans generally—not unlike the emperors at Rome's Coliseum. In the Bismarck Hotel, one of the family's vast real estate holdings, Bill had his own private meeting/dining rooms. His personal car was a limousine which he drove himself.

The NHL was a democratic organization of hockey team owners. Bill was a member and he enjoyed more clout than other members. In *Animal Farm*, novelist George Orwell wrote that when the pigs took over rule of all the barnyard animals they modified the ruling premise, 'All animals are equal' by adding the phrase, 'but some animals are more equal than others.'"

On occasion, Bill's requests to Commissioner Clarence Campbell were treated as the unanimous vote of the league.

Indeed, the Blackhawks were virtually a fiefdom of the Wirtz family. Imagine: grim organ music selected by Bill's wife.

This is not an indictment of Bill as a person or even as a boss. While notoriously reluctant to pay up for top players, he was amazingly beneficent to those on his team, always there to help them and their families in joy and in sorrow, even paying for the wake of Keith Magnuson, long retired player and coach.

This is intended to reflect on a man of contradictions perhaps, but certainly a man entrenched and comfortable in his royal cocoon. A man above, and certainly not of, the people.

A man whose views were adamant, whose opinions were expressed in words spoken softly but heard loud, even if cloaked in the silent treatment a la Rocky. He was a man who felt he could afford to ignore his constituents. Sports fans are notorious for expressing their opinions. But when it came to Bill Wirtz, potential critics inside and outside the company realized that expressing their wishes would be, let us say, like a Roman citizen telling a Caesar which gladiator to send to the lions.

Vision: The Rocky Wirtz Mystique

There were many changes: when the various stakeholders saw that Rocky was bringing in people who were accessible, they began to move in his direction.

Rocky was fully immersed in the process and addressed matters both large and not so large: "I'm in the open; I sit in regular seats, not in a sky box.

"One day, a fellow stopped me. He had two seats near us and wanted to move up one row. He said the Blackhawk office said Dad had a hold on the seats, yet there was never anyone in them."

Ultimately, Rocky worked with the man and sold him four tickets where he wanted to be, instead of the two that he had. In recognizing that this fan was right, he doubled his business with this customer, a kind of risk-reward meme for Rocky. [Wirtz #11]

It's truly difficult to imagine what it was like for the Blackhawks organization in 2007 when Bill died and Peter quit. The organization's attitude embodied assumptions: that income didn't matter because the Blackhawks team was the Wirtz family hobby; that customers - the fans, media, advertisers, the community - could be ignored. In fact, fans should be grateful that the Wirtz family was willing to keep the Blackhawks in Chicago, even though few fans remained who really cared.

The employee attitude reflected disappointment with the management point of view. The lack of TV coverage resulted in distracting phone calls that vexed idle sales folk. Why bother? The good news was there was no animosity between the Blackhawks and the media. The bad news was that the lack of animosity was because there was simply no relationship between the parties whatsoever.

Rocky Wirtz was all business, based on his no-nonsense sales and marketing background. Perhaps he's not as extreme as "the customer is always right," but certainly he's well beyond ignoring the customer. His sales orientation and sensitivities—go to the customer's place of business where he feels comfortable and at an advantage, listen to his needs, and create a win-win solution—were embedded in his vision, which was the perfect potion for what ailed the team.

Rocky also had a family business perspective. He had suffered through years of knowing that under his grandfather's will he would eventually lead the family's businesses. Yet he was kept at bay, not allowed to join his brother and father when they discussed the Blackhawks. He was not privy to the financials – and they reflected abysmal results. He lacked opportunity for input while sitting in the family's "penalty box." He did succeed two dynamic businessmen—his grandfather and his father—who had built an empire with impressive growth in spirits, real estate and banking.

(Eventually, Rocky was to discover that there also were challenges and opportunities in the real estate, spirits and banking segments as well. All proved solvable.)

Despite all that, he was able to devise a way to win over his stakeholders/constituents. And then he was able to implant his vision in them. It wasn't easy. But with clever sales approaches, by showing he was serious about driving the team to the Stanley Cup, by dropping the 'royal family' image and consulting with customers personally, it all came together.

Leaders Must Have a Vision, Not Necessarily That of the Followers

There was no reason for anyone to expect change when Bill died. After all, the essence of a dynasty is that things stay the same. Successors reign in much the same way as their fathers, living in the same castle with the same moat.

Rocky never viewed himself as part of the dynasty. Indeed, he should have had trouble viewing himself as part of his family, a family that shut him out and later sued him.

Yet he felt an obligation to the family. He simply didn't feel obliged to be like them or to think like them. It couldn't have been easy to strike out so differently, to abandon his family's bizarre rules, to cease being part of dynastic tradition and to mingle with the real people, hear their anguish, feel their pain, give them what they needed and what they felt they deserved.

But in fact, it *was* easy. His decisions and actions were the product of his visions, that the Blackhawks weren't the Wirtz's hobby, and that if it were, it was too expensive a hobby for him and his family. In any event, the hockey business needed a good marketing and sales approach to be profitable, which was the compelling goal for Rocky.

▼▼▼▼▼▼▼▼▼▼▼▼▼▼▼▼▼▼▼▼▼▼▼▼▼▼▼▼▼▼▼▼▼▼▼▼▼▼

Two Visions: Only One Visible

Perhaps the full irony of the extent to which Rocky's vision carried the organization can be found in the following story. In 2009, the Blackhawks began a program to urge their couch potato fans to watch the games at their local "Official Blackhawks Bars." It's a great marketing gimmick. It's also a great irony. This was team that prevented fans from watching games on TV, in a foolhardy attempt to fill the stands, necessitating giving free tickets for players to hand out in order to have some fans at the arena. Then a change of vision, and games transmitted on TV motivated the fans to fill the stadium. Non-existent marketing, due to a vision guided by parsimony and segregated divisions, yielded to a vision that to build a business requires investment and enterprise cross marketing. Now, three Stanley Cups later, the United Center is always full. Fans can't get (or afford) tickets. Cleverly wanting to have ever-more committed fans, they devised the "Official Blackhawks Bars" program, giving fans rewards for watching Blackhawks games at bars rather than at home. Brilliant! It demonstrates how Rocky's "Beyond-the-Eaves" vision was not just to rebuild the team but also to do what he complained his father and brother wouldn't do, namely cross-fertilize between the Wirtz's hockey team interests and their booze distribution business, now known as Breakthru Beverage Group. [Wirtz #12]

▲▲▲▲▲▲▲▲▲▲▲▲▲▲▲▲▲▲▲▲▲▲▲▲▲▲▲▲▲▲▲▲▲▲▲▲▲▲

THE VISION THING

The Can-Do Leadership of Rocky Wirtz

The Chicago Blackhawks were on death watch when Rocky took over. He found players were owed $40 million in compensation. He paid. His goal:

win the Stanley Cup for a dispirited team that filled a mere 3,400 paid seats. Rocky's leadership skill let him hire (sans pay hike) a team manager who had been able to continue making money with the hapless Cubs. Rocky got ad buyers to vie for oceans of unsold TV space and got newspapers to cover away games even before the team began to win again. Girded with new stars and Rocky's vision, the Blackhawks did come back and repaid his novel leadership path many times over. The Stanley Cup? Yes!

It worked so well that the picture I portrayed in the first paragraph of this chapter—that of Rocky smiling broadly as he raised the Cup over his head—has been repeated twice as the Blackhawks won the Stanley Cup again in 2013 and 2015. Oh yes, the Blackhawks have raised ticket prices in each of the last six years as of this writing. [Wirtz #13]

Rocky knew the Blackhawks couldn't survive if his father's vision were to prevail. He was confident that his own goal was achievable. Indeed, Forest & Trees Vision told Rocky his goal had always been within reach, but only with a new approach. It wasn't that Bill couldn't have focused on revenue growth. He was a smart and capable guy. He simply chose not to do so.

VISION CHART

(For Chapter One)

▶ It's OK to have different visions in each generation and over time.

▶ When your family business vision is to sustain a big-boy's hobby, it's appropriate to focus on costs: How expensive a hobby can I afford? When the vision is to increase long-term value, focus may be better aimed at revenue.

▶ What comes first, family or business, is a critical issue for a visionary. The two are not necessarily mutually exclusive. All of us are capable of being both family and business visionaries. Understand your goals and capabilities before trying to formulate your vision.

The Vision Transition

When the time comes for a dramatic change in the direction of a family business a new generation is often key to success. Rocky Wirtz changed the financial emphasis of the Blackhawks to save a dying enterprise. On a different track, Eli's Cheesecake moved from a dad's vision for an iconic restaurant dessert to his son's vision of the confection as a treat on the national market.

CHAPTER 2

Eli Schulman

When it Comes to Desserts Marc & Eli Take the Cheesecake

▼▼▼▼▼▼▼▼▼▼▼

*E*li Schulman had been in the restaurant business since he established *Eli's Ogden* Huddle before World War II. *This morphed into* Eli's Stage Delicatessen just off Chicago's Loop, *a "go to" destination for the city's in-crowd: top politicos, business moguls, TV hosts and columnists, not to mention stars like Woody Allen and Barbra Streisand. Eli the host was "schmoozer-in-chief" and wanted to scale but could not meet and greet in two hot spots at the same time. That's assuming he could in fact make two eateries work. Few can. But son Marc scaled the business, filling the corporate menu with dessert to create a sweet legacy.*

An Eponymous First Name

Eli Schulman grew up on Chicago's west side. Friends from the west side who became successful entrepreneurs, powerful politicians and media personalities, were helpful through the numerous iterations of Eli's business.

In 1966, Eli Schulman progressed from homey deli to posh tablecloth draped, *Eli's: The Place for Steak.* Eli had been in the restaurant business since he established *Eli's Ogden Huddle* in Chicago in 1940. This was to become *Eli's Stage Delicatessen*, just off Chicago's Loop, a "go to" attraction for top politicians, business moguls like Bill Wrigley and Charlie Lubin of Sara Lee fame; noted Second City columnists and television hosts like locally-famous Irv (Kup) Kupcinet, along with lots of star entertainers, including Sammy Davis, Jr. and Henny Youngman. Eli took the crowd with him to *Eli's: The Place for Steak,* and the restaurant thrived. Eli was always there, greeting and providing his distinctive welcome to Chicago's rich and famous: also to world-famed Frank Sinatra, who gave Schulman a watch Eli would flash with pride. In short he loved each minute of this. [Schulman #1]

He also planned the menu. That wasn't difficult, since return customers favored his signature dishes: Calves Liver Eli, Shrimp Dejonghe and the traditional Eli's Steaks. That having been said, Eli was not oblivious to the advantages of scaling in business. Eli worked long hours. At times he'd stick around until 1:00 a.m. to close up. His son, Marc, has said, "There's nothing worse than just sitting in the restaurant until you lock the door." [Schulman #2]

Yes, restaurants are a tough business. The hours are long, customers are demanding, staff tends not to be dependable and inventories are perishable. Patrons are fickle, too: they switch allegiances to newer dining places or stray to seek novel cuisine.

Some restaurateurs seek to scale by opening additional locations and even different restaurants. Eli Schulman didn't want that. My guess is he was too fond of greeting "the royalty," of making famous friends, not just being host. The wristwatch given to him by Sinatra gave him an icon's stamp of approval.

He couldn't be in two places at one time and certainly wouldn't have wanted to miss greeting Barbra or Sammy or any of his other special guests when they came to a restaurant of his.

Eli Schulman needed to scale differently: food items, not multiple restaurants. The popularity of his signature dishes suggested his skill set ran in the direction of creating outstanding food products. Why not a signature dessert? In the back of his mind was that scaling prospect: "if I can create a signature dessert, perhaps it can be sold on a broader basis."

As confirmed by son Marc, it's likely he was thinking in terms of the local market: Perhaps he could get restaurateur friends to add his inspired cheesecake to their menus or get a local supermarket to carry it in the refrigerated food section.

Limited in scope, perhaps: that was Eli's vision. He pursued the vision slowly, even tentatively. After all, the restaurant was supporting himself and his wife. That had to be his primary focus. Still, cheesecake might be his avenue to the heavens, not just the stars.

His son, Marc, a lawyer with a transactional practice in a top Chicago law firm, regarded his own work as unexciting. So he joined the business some years before Eli died in 1988. Marc was named president of the company in 1984. Meantime, Eli's Original Plain Cheesecake had become a Chicago hit. Eli's lush cheesecake is made of cream cheese, sour cream, eggs, sugar, and vanilla in a butter shortbread cookie crust.

▼▼▼▼▼▼▼▼▼▼▼▼▼▼▼▼▼▼▼▼▼▼▼▼▼▼▼▼▼▼▼▼▼

First Name First Beats Dessert Before Dinner

Family business leadership succession has many complicating factors and burdens. One seeming advantage is the benefit of name recognition. The family name can create a solid foundation, upon which succession and successors can build and grow. Especially for eponymous companies named after their founder. That advantage is tied to the family name. Other eponymous businesses based on family name: Ford. Mars, Tiffany, Chanel, Wrigley, Perot Systems, and of course, Trump.

Importance of family name recognition faded as Marc's father's 'given name' recognition grew by leaps and bounds. It grew even though Marc's father died in 1988. After all, Marc's father was Eli Schulman, and their successful family business was built around Eli's Cheesecake. Other 'given name' firms that started as restaurants: Nathan's Famous (hot dogs) and Bob Evan's (sausage). Ben & Jerry's began as an Ice Cream store.

Beware The Optimist: With Eyes Bigger Than His Appetite

When a successful company spawns a new business, serious decisions must be made. How real are the inevitable "amazing" prospects projected for any new business, and how much time, money and personal attention will it take? Important questions, these.

How much of the firm's precious resources can the main business do without before feeling the cost or worse?

Such measurements are difficult and usually impossible to make with any degree of accuracy. Often the decisions are made emotionally. It is said that nature abhors (and will fill) a vacuum. A lack of substantiated facts creates a vacuum that tends to be filled by emotions. While some emotion-based business decisions are good, most are not. In any event, such decisions defy typical business measurements.

Eli created his iconic cheesecake in the late 1970s. In *Eli's: The Place for Steak, Eli's Cheesecake* was easily the favorite dessert. Even so, in the wholesale market, sales grew slowly for a while.

Then in 1980, Mayor Jane Byrne, a friend of Eli, founded Taste of Chicago, a food fair serving 'walk-by' patrons samples of morsels sold in Chicago eateries. It has since become a huge festival, hosting over a million every year and culminating with the city's July 4 fireworks display. In 1980 it was to be small and held between two Michigan Ave. buildings: But the crowd was twice the 100,000 expected. Eli's cheesecake was relatively new, and still mostly sold only at *Eli's: The Place For Steak*. Eli's cake was one of 36 featured foods. Today, *Eli's Cheesecake* is the only one of those 36 foods still in business with the same ownership participating in last year's fair, which hosted nearly 1.5 million guests. *Eli's Cheesecake* was a hit. After all, what's not to like?

▼▼▼▼▼▼▼▼▼▼▼▼▼▼▼▼▼▼▼▼▼▼▼▼▼▼▼▼

The Adoptive Lure of A Father's Vision

In 1980, Marc was still practicing law at a prominent downtown Chicago law firm. He had experienced Alfie-like thoughts, as found in the lyrics of "What's it All About, Alfie?," the Burt Bacharach/Hal David song made famous by the movie, *Alfie*. Marc had previously considered becoming a deputy commissioner of housing in Mayor Jane Byrne's administration. But now he was having thoughts of a more exciting endeavor.

His parents were getting older: he relished the opportunity to work alongside them. If Eli's cheesecake vision were to become reality, his parents would need help. His father's reluctance to bring in investors limited prospects for growth.

Marc's transactional law practice involved fleeting relationships at best. Happily married Marc preferred long-term relationships. He considered time an investment in doing things right. After all, who would microwave a cheesecake?

Also, he remembered *Little Jack's* Restaurant, an extremely popular dining room on Chicago's west side in the 1940s and 1950s. This successful business closed when the neighborhood changed. Few remember *Little Jack's* now, except for the small number remaining who had frequented it back then. Marc craved something enduring.

While his last name and father's relationships could lead to business in the practice of law and to the benefits that accrue to law firm rainmakers, there could possibly be greater value in his father's first name and the more direct legacies of his father's vision via *Eli's: The Place for Steak* and *Eli's Cheesecake*.

Ah, that vision. Could it be adopted by Marc? Could the company be adapted to enable true and serious scaling of the cheesecake business without damaging the restaurant, which already was the financial support of both of Marc's parents?

If he joined, there was the added burden of supporting Marc and his family. Last but certainly not least: did Marc have sufficient talent and skill to do both? And if successfully adopted, could the cheesecake vision be adapted to scale?

Marc decided that it was the right time—now or never. "Now or never" turned out to be accurate. Just a few years later, Eli died. The restaurant remained open, run by Marc and his mother, for another 17 years, until the building was demolished and became the site for the Lurie Children's Hospital.

▲▲▲▲▲▲▲▲▲▲▲▲▲▲▲▲▲▲▲▲▲▲▲▲▲▲▲▲▲▲▲

Shortly after Marc joined the family business and not long before Eli died, Chicagoans were mesmerized by the success of Mike Ditka's Chicago Bears. The extraordinary team—Walter Payton, Jim McMahon, Mike Singletary, and The Fridge—were going to the Super Bowl and were becoming darlings of the media with the video of their Super Bowl Shuffle antics.

As is the annual custom, the mayors of the cities playing in the Super Bowl made a friendly and civic-oriented wager on the outcome of the game. If the Patriots lost, Mayor Raymond Flynn of Boston would send Chicago's Mayor Harold Washington two live lobsters and a quantity of New England clam chowder.

And if the Bears lost, Mayor Washington would send to Mayor Flynn a package consisting of several of Chicago's signal ethnic neighborhood foods and—what else?—*Eli's Cheesecake.*

Back then, in Chicago, when 'da Mayor' promoted your product, doors opened. When the promotion, by two mayors, is connected with Taste of Chicago and the only Super Bowl victory of 'da Bears', well, only the Cubs selecting Eli's Cheesecake over champagne after winning the World Series could be bigger.

Marc grabbed the *Eli's Cheesecake* ball and ran with it. Not even Chicago's famed running back Walter Payton could've done better. (Payton was called "Sweetness," somewhat like the essence of *Eli's Cheesecake*). Eli's vision was adopted by Marc who reconfigured it, expanding it to global proportions.

Eli's vision was constrained by his emotional need to be a full time meeter-and-greeter of the rich and famous, which enabled the steakhouse to pay the bills. Marc's vision was borne in moderation. He knew: to achieve his vision, he had to break with his father's.

Unrestrained by not needing to be an on-hand greeter at the restaurant, Marc focused on cheesecake. He caused the company to adapt, increasing the size of the premises devoted to the cheesecake operation. Later, in 1996, Marc built a large, modern bakery plant to house it.

Today, *Eli's Cheesecake* is sold in every state in the United States and in 10 other countries. They have over 25,000 doors selling their cakes (cheesecake remains the firm's top product) and overall, *Eli's Cheesecake* sells 300,000 portions per day.

A few months before Eli's death, the family threw him a birthday party. The attendees were a Who's Who list of Chicago luminaries, among others, prominent judges (Hon. Abe Marovitz), former governors (Jim Thompson), former prosecutors (Dan Webb and Anton Valukas), columnist and TV host, Irv ("Kup") Kupcinet, and many more.

This was just two years after the Super Bowl; four years after Marc joined the business. There was progress but nothing like what was to come. But Eli liked what he saw. He was proud of how Marc had begun his adaptive process for the firm, and he said, to a top Sara Lee executive, "Hey, you know what? My son and our business are going in the right direction." Sweet!

THE VISION THING

Marc's Vision for *Eli's Cheesecake*

Restaurateurs with a first establishment doing well often open a second outlet and more. Most find that success in the first outlet is generally a poor indicator of success in more than one.

Often the burden of running two units negatively impacts both. The new store folds and the successful one flops too.

They find that "one-off "success is merely a sign of one skill set unlike those needed to run multiple restaurants.

Of course, some do have that second skill set. Chicagoans such as Arnie Morton (*Morton's*), Gene Sage (*Sage's*), and Richie Melman (*Lettuce Entertain You*) Restaurants are prime examples of successful scaling. All were friends of Eli.

Other restaurateurs who found Melman and Morton to be compelling role models with amazing track records took the plunge only to discover that scaling restaurants is not easy.

Eli's vision was scaled to his own skill set. He measured his success by his presence in his restaurant as host. He turned to his bakery and created a cheesecake to die for—initially to enhance and attract loyal patrons of his restaurant and later, tentatively, to sell through some Chicago friends' channels.

Marc adopted his father's vision as to the product but not the channel of distribution. Trending Pattern Vision told Marc that there was an approachable runway for his big vision to take off. His big vision was selling Eli's Cheesecake all over the country and even around the world.

VISION CHART

(For Chapter 2)

▶ Lifestyle choices such as the desire to rub elbows with the Sinatras of the world affect vision, just as the vision of moving cheesecake into food stores) can affect lifestyle choices. Decide which you can live with and which you cannot live without.

▶ Relinquishing a professional career with attendant status and security, to pursue a vision, especially someone else's vision, takes exceptional commitment to the vision but can be both necessary and worthwhile. Understand what's really important to you.

The Vision Transition

The five elements of visions I propose are silos across a horizontal spectrum, intended to organize analyses of visionaries. Each of them can be applied to the vertical segments so familiar to businesspeople: sourcing, purchasing, production, marketing and sales, including channels, etc.

Both Schulman visions were profitable. Thus, their respective visions were successful. Profit is the name of the game. No enterprise can survive if losses build on losses without profit at some point. This applies to corporations run for profit and to not-for-profits like Underwriters Laboratories. CEO Keith Williams did not have the luxury of earnings to cushion the fading fortunes of Underwriters Laboratories. Set up to validate the safety of US manufactured products, UL was a prestige non-profit. But Williams had to remind a capable but self-satisfied staff that perpetual losses kill businesses – even not-for-profits. The visionary new CEO found novel ways to battle a welter of profit motivated rivals. Read on to measure his success.

CHAPTER 3

Keith Williams

UL's Seal of Approval
Led to Hobbling Losses:
Enter Keith Williams

▼▼▼▼▼▼▼▼▼▼▼▼

*U*nderwriters Laboratories (UL) had a rich and important history. For over a hundred years it provided valuable services. That UL label affixed to electric appliances after safety testing virtually forced manufacturers of electronic appliances to spend the time and money to prevent fires and explosions that previously had been caused by their products. But its world changed. UL had become complacent when Keith Williams arrived to change it from non-profit to profit seeker. Would this be possible? Touch and go without a new vision to be sure.

Does Doing Good Necessitate
Not Doing Well?

In the years preceding fire retardant materials in home construction, electric appliances seemed no safer than kerosene lamps, coal stoves and similar products they were replacing.

Through good science and engineering, discipline and creativity, UL revolutionized the industry and was singly responsible for making homes and work places safer. Without the UL emblem, indicating inspection and certification of compliance with safety rules, manufacturers found it difficult at best to obtain the insurance that was a prerequisite to securing customers and outlets for their products.

UL became a virtual monopoly and was showered with praise and support from all sectors, including the U.S. Congress.

If ever a company seemed like it could coast along effortlessly forever, UL might have been that company.

Yet in 2005, when Keith Williams entered the spacious offices high atop the UL headquarters in Northbrook, Illinois, even as he looked down on the well-manicured lawns of the vast UL property below, he knew that UL's days of coasting were decidedly over.

Indeed, it was by no means clear that UL could be saved. It didn't take Keith long to understand why: UL was living under the auspices of an outmoded vision. He would have to create a new vision immediately, and that was no small challenge.

Keith was noted for his deftness at turning around troubled businesses. But this situation was different and would require unique approaches.

A quick appraisal of UL's non-financial assets and liabilities convinced Williams that UL still had great values. They clearly were "the good guys," responsible for saving incalculable lives and property. In their own way, the UL team caused U.S. manufacturers to elevate the quality of their products and simultaneously to improve their long-term operating results. As one UL employee put it to Williams: "We were kind of like the government."

The company took great pains to prevent conflicts of interest which otherwise seemed inevitable, given their businesses. Originally founded by the National Board of Fire Underwriters, they became independent in 1936. Still, they set the standards and then charged companies for certifying compliance with those standards. But internal controls were established to prevent conflicts. When a safety standard is developed by UL, everyone can use it, including competitors.

Keith believed it would be fundamentally wrong for UL to certify products where they also provided design advisory services. So they refrain from providing design services in those situations. They explain to clients that they cannot do that and offer instead to educate the company on compliance.

Keith also quickly determined that UL had an extremely talented and experienced cadre of scientists and engineers who unfortunately had traveled without effective leadership, into an attitudinal abyss: they actually believed that UL could go on forever without making a profit.

The same employees who wondered why UL needed to make a profit also asked why it was necessary to have a sales force. After all, if customers want our services, they will come to us, right? (Further proof that "Build it, and they will come" is more appropriate in the world of fiction.) [Williams #1]

A Not-For-Profit Business? Not Really

How did such smart people come to such a ridiculous conclusion? To some extent this probably resulted from a misunderstanding about its essential form.

Most businesses operate through a corporation that is owned by shareholders who are entitled to all the company's income and the proceeds of any sale of their shares.

Certain businesses operate as not-for-profit corporations. UL is, of course, one of these. The not-for-profit has no shareholders. The company's income can only be used for its business and cannot ever be distributed to anyone. Since there are no shareholders, in a liquidation for whatever reason, a court or government agency will determine what to do with the company's assets. But the proceeds will not inure to any individual's benefit.

In certain circumstances, the not-for-profit company can run charitable operations that receive earnings accruing from its non-profit operations. A good example of that would be not-for-profit hospitals. These are the most profitable hospitals, yet most do charitable work such as caring for the poor. Ergo, a not-for-profit business is still a business whose goal is to make a profit.

The phrase "not-for-profit" relates to the individuals involved, not to the company. No individual can gain owner's profit from such a business. Some not-for-profits aim at spending all their profits in support of their functions and causes. Those companies typically have external sources of funding, such as charitable contributions by those supporting their goals. But many not-for-profit companies depend on internal profit as a goal, to continue their existence and growth.

A famous group of not-for-profit businesses are the Blue Cross-Blue Shield insurance companies. They have been extremely profitable but have no distributions to owners because they have no shareholders. Profits are plowed back into the business, enabling extraordinary growth and, some might say, unfair advantage.

All this is distinguishable but not totally dissimilar to the perception of the Blackhawks Hockey Team (a for-profit organization) as a family hobby with continual losses.

▲▲▲▲▲▲▲▲▲▲▲▲▲▲▲▲▲▲▲▲▲▲▲▲▲▲▲▲▲▲▲▲▲▲▲

Underwriter Laboratories was founded as a not-for-profit business in 1894. Manufactures whose products had the famous UL insignia, indicating compliance with UL's strict standards, had a serious competitive advantage. For nearly a century, UL's not-for-profit status gave it unique credibility and its own competitive advantage.

Arrogance in business tends to destroy motivation. The resulting complacence can lead to disaster. You'll recall examples in which market share becomes so large that it spawns a lackadaisical attitude: "We virtually own the market, so we really don't have to try harder." Well, imagine what happens if you really own the entire market.

Ninety plus years of superiority, of skilled employees, and of well-developed relationships in government and industry, pretty much eliminated and precluded competition. In 1953 UL's relationships and golden reputation paid off: friends in the U.S. Congress passed a special law freeing UL of having to pay income taxes. That was reasonable. UL had a noble purpose: protecting consumers from dangerous products.

After World War II, consumer spending on household appliances grew phenomenally as a result of pent-up demand dampened by the Great Depression and war. Suddenly that demand was released by the burgeoning homebuilding fostered by a flood of mortgages fostered under the G.I. Bill of Rights.

America needed UL, so why not help them? The Act didn't actually name UL. It would have covered any company that did what UL did; there simply wasn't any such company in 1953. There have been many definitions of monopoly over the years. Underwriters Laboratories—UL—fit all those definitions then.

And that led to malaise and a feeling of "no need to make a profit." Clueless: like the banditos in *The Treasure of Sierra Madre* film who tried to seize the prospectors' gold? Bogart asked to see their badges. To that the oafish sombrero clad Jefe shrieked, "Badges? We don't need no stinking badges!"

Perhaps the UL team misunderstood the term "not-for-profit." Either way, the combined effect of their lack of effort to get more business or create new services the customers craved, caused Underwriters Laboratories to dip into its reserves.

At about that time, three events occurred. First, competitors arrived on the scene, some offering the new services customers wanted but couldn't get from UL; others offered services directly competitive with UL's. Second, more and more things were being manufactured elsewhere, a trend started by America's inability to compete with cheap labor and more efficient factories abroad. Third, UL's monopoly was diluted in the last years of the 20th century when OSHA created a program called Nationally Recognized Testing Laboratories.

The NRTL program said that anyone who was accredited by OSHA could issue certifications like UL's. That brought in a lot of competition, and UL really struggled to adapt to that.

Each of the UL labs around the world, including those in the United States, was essentially an independent P&L center, so they were competing with each other for business. Worst of all, UL was "a one act play" as Williams described it. "We were 'safety certification' only, and customers were buying more and more of a range of other services: performance testing, pre-shipment inspecting, vendor qualification, etc. UL was really becoming more and more of a niche supplier."

All that was capped by the sucking sound of manufacturing jobs going to Mexico, as Ross Perot warned as a candidate for president of the United States in 1992 (see Chapter 6). Jobs going to China caused a cyclone by comparison. UL began bleeding cash. While financial results weren't shared with all employees, "they knew there was a problem," Williams said.

"The company had sold some of its assets to raise cash. So the people knew it was bad, and yet…it was someone else's problem, management or the Board. They were kind of looking for leadership in terms of how they could fix the problem."

Complacency had proved more powerful than an Act of Congress at eliminating any income tax simply by eliminating any income. And as assets were sold, the reserves were further depleted. UL was definitely in trouble.

After the turn to the 21st-century, the need to fix things became obvious. A new CEO, prior to Keith Williams' tenure, was brought in to fix things. That CEO—the first outsider in the position—started with layoffs and other cost-cutting efforts. This reduced but did not stop the bleeding. In fact, the layoffs proved detrimental to effecting a turnaround, as sufficiently skilled replacements for the laid off folks were difficult to find.

We'll never know whether he could have done it; illness caused a premature departure, his potential untapped.

That's when UL brought in Keith Williams, an experienced and talented turnaround artist. Keith had spent years out of the U.S. and most recently several years in Japan. That "foreign service" had sensitized Keith to the role of dealing with different cultures. In those years, even more than now, the differences between national cultures were extreme. Keith was up to the job but faced extreme challenges in the UL culture.

One shouldn't confuse culture with values and goals. Fortunately, Keith was not confused. UL's values and goals were sound. UL had a great history of science and public safety. UL had made a huge contribution to society.

Keith feels "the most valuable thing we have is the mission, the sense of purpose—working for a safer world. That's incredibly valuable. We want to retain that as our core. We also want to be a modern competitive company because the second thing that's important to us is our independence: If we fail commercially, then we lose our independence."

UL's culture had been failing: "Along the way [we] started to become very insular; bureaucratic. When you have a very strong position in the market and especially when you are the only one in the market, it can change your attitude from service to something else. We had a very unhappy customer base, a very unhappy employee base, and started losing a lot of market share to competition. Most urgent was the attitude of 'We are kind of like a government agency, which means people have to listen to what we say. And oh by the way, there's no requirement to make a profit.' The culture I found here was really a command and control culture. The people had become blind followers."

UL's vision had truly become distorted: It didn't seem to know what it was—let alone what it wanted to be.

Keith had his own vision for UL. His vision clashed with UL's culture. Retro Vision identified the company's values and the strength of its brand. Beyond-the-Eaves Vision showed him competitors' encroachment on UL's market share. Trend Pattern Vision showed dire consequences were imminent. Forest & Trees Vision exposed the gap between employees' attitudes and reality, as well as their great skills despite their misguided attitudes.

His vision was of a UL that continued its capabilities but with goals of profit through expansion of business both new and existing. He started doing weekly emails to all of the employees, which of course initiated a lot of feedback.

He also instituted numerous training programs. UL spent two thirds of its educational budget on technical training and one third on leadership training. That was disproportionate in that 85 percent of employees were technical and 15 percent were in leadership. It served Keith's purpose to focus on leadership training, because that was the best way to reshape the culture of the organization.

Other training programs stressed a rationalized pricing structure to get people accustomed to the idea that making money is OK.[Williams #2] Keith said:

"Even your local house-of-worship, whatever religion you may be involved in, actually has to have a surplus of revenues over expenses. Otherwise, how do you build the next house of worship or repair the one you have, if all you're doing is covering your cost, right? After all, whether you're enriching some individuals or enriching society, everybody has to make money." Of course, the house-of-worship likely receives tithes or contributions. Such "pay to pray" contributions are a form of revenue. [Williams #3]

In addition to Keith's weekly update emails, which he still sends a decade later, the CFO records a quarterly briefing, followed by a personal hour long report, held in Northbrook's cafeteria but transmitted on the internet to UL people globally.

It's recorded to serve different time zones and to reach employees who travel. Williams said these communications "also talk about happy and unhappy customers, as well as other things that are happening in the business. There is conversation about why we need to be in a particular business, and we talk about business culture too." [Williams #4]

Keith determined that UL had to provide the various services that its customers wanted. However, it did not do this in a willy-nilly fashion. If it knew something about the industry and could add a new client category, it would do it.

New service capabilities were added similarly. Or if it had a service-base that it knew well, it could add a new industry or a new client base. However, if it knew nothing about the industry and nothing about the technology, then it would not enter the prospective business segment.

UL began to make acquisitions: It has acquired approximately 35 companies since 2008, at a cost of over $1 billion in cash. [Williams #5] The cash was generated from operations since 2005. There was no cash before Keith arrived. The businesses have included advisory services, energy efficiency testing, color spectrum rating, biological hazard testing, and many others.

Further expansion related to electronic payment security in another core business, namely, life and health certifying.

This led to other services in the health care industry. For example, UL provided electrical safety certification for things like x-ray machines. From that it was able to offer advisory service for things such as ergonomics, to lend a human factor to medical devices. Once there, it was able to guide people in regulatory filings and submissions. UL actually trains the FDA but also trains customers on how to work with the FDA process.

Additionally, it bought an environmental company that does indoor air quality testing. There is a need for safety and material sourcing related to all kinds of chemical components in the world. UL now has companies that source materials to bring safety data sheets to market.

Most of the company's acquisitions were successful entrepreneurial companies. Keith wanted to keep the profit-driven entrepreneurial culture alive. Wherever possible, he retained management and specifically asked them "Please keep your culture and help us teach that to the rest of the company."

THE VISION THING

Keith Williams' Sweeping Vision Turned Around UL

UL's old structure was a 501(c)(3) not-for-profit. As they started acquiring companies, it arranged for separate for-profit corporations to make those acquisitions. However, each for-profit company is 100% owned by the not-for-profit company. [Williams #6]

It no longer was concerned about taxes, since it was pretty much paying taxes for everything it did outside the U.S. Testing for public safety occurred primarily in the U.S.

Having the for-profit companies gave UL the ability, in the future, if needed, to access public markets or certain kinds of private markets for money and to reduce reliance on debt.

While it is possible someday in the future for stock to be distributed to employees, currently all stock is owned by the not-for-profit company. As a result there are no real owners.

Keith was concerned about public perception. What if people thought the reorganization was being done to benefit insiders? That's why he was very careful to structure the reorganization in a way that prevented officers or directors from receiving any of the equity.

While employees cannot own stock in the company, UL has created an all-employee incentive program that uses peer pressure plus dollars in pocket to motivate employees to do what's important for the business to succeed. This is just another example of management trying to create more of a real business with a commercial orientation for the company, in other words, tactics and strategy driven by vision. [Williams #7]

According to Keith, one of the most important things UL had was their mission, the sense of purpose, working for a safer world. That mission had several iterations over time but it's a real motivator to people. It's incredibly valuable in that respect and something they struggle to retain as part of its core.

At the same time UL's people wanted it to be a modern competitive company, because independence was very important to its mission, and if it failed commercially, then the people knew they would lose their independence. When Keith Williams envisioned the future for UL, he saw UL's values as the basis for building that future.

There is perhaps no better example of Trend Pattern Vision than Keith's vision of UL's changing needs and purposes as the 20th century turned into the 21st. In the 20th century, electrical safety and fire safety were critical public safety issues of the time. His vision for the 21st-century is that it's going to be chemical and environmental safety, as well as cyber security.

VISION CHART

(For Chapter 3)

▶ Don't confuse the *mission* to improve the safety of all the appliances in the market place, with the necessary *vision* to continually modify the mission to survive in an increasingly competitive environment.

▶ Don't allow artificial rules (not-for-profit entities) to interfere with your business vision.

▶ When your people have the correct vision but a distorted sense of reality, fix the unreal perception.

▶ Never argue with someone's beliefs when you can argue with their knowledge, because most people believe far more than they know.

The Vision Transition

In UL, Keith used Retro Vision to banish old do-good values. This made it possible for him to eradicate faulty visions that emanated from the arrogance of monopoly.

The Underwriters Labs story is extreme. UL needed a vision to change a company's culture from accepting losses to recognizing that profits are needed to survive. Now let's consider a challenge only slightly different: an industry happy to operate with margins so slim that a penny price change would have proved devastating in the jug wine business.

CHAPTER 4

Tony and Bill Terlato

Terlato Family Sips a Path to Vintage Extraordinaire

▼▼▼▼▼▼▼▼▼▼▼▼

*T*he Terlato family entered the wine business in the USA when jug wine was a near commodity product. Earn a few cents per jug or raise the price per gallon one penny and lose market share. Anthony Terlato felt Americans were ready for a better product. That vision of Americans choosing fine wines gave him the confidence to risk it all. His decision proved correct, but son, Bill, felt vulnerable to wine producers. That led Bill to convert the family business to include growing and vintnering. His vision changed the business, a tribute to his good taste. Bill's vision was built on the foundation of his dad's vision. Good visions in successive generations. Result: Terlato wines are cherished bottles in dining house wine cellars. For the Terlatos it's like "vino, vidi, vici" - wine vision conquers all.

A Leader Must Have a Vision

Terlato Wine Company's Bill Terlato knew he must have a vision for his family's wine company if he were to lead it: People only follow a leader when they think he has "vision and capability and can bring them to a better place."

Bill's vision for Terlato Wines appears at first blush to be much the same as the vision of his father, Anthony (Tony) Terlato. But that's anything but a coincidence. It's a result of their hard work, Tony's structured mentoring, and the fierce dedication of both Terlatos. Their efforts were part of their succession plan, another 'vision' that Tony wisely conceived when Bill was a young boy. While their visions appear identical—develop and sell high quality wines to Americans—appearances can be confusing. Thus, close evaluation shows their visions are dramatically different. Their two stories will help you see why.

Bottling Up and Relabeling Old Visions

Where do visions go when a business leader, either the original visionary or a successor leader, has a new vision (or a re-vision, if you will)? Some visions may disappear instantly. Most, however, taper and fade over a period of time, leaving a vacuum to be filled by the successor vision. How well the new vision fills that gap, how well it provides a lantern by which the new leader can see the future may determine the speed with which the old vision fades. If circumstances have made the old vision irrelevant, then there is ample room for the new vision. In that case, the old vision may go from being an aspiration to becoming a mere former policy or goal. Such a transformation—with respect for the old vision and passion for the new— can be healthy for the future of the business.

During the transition, the company may well have more than one vision, one ebbing while the other is flowing. That requires attention to and nurturing of both. Like any distraction, such an outcome can create a burden. A lot depends on the culture of the organization and the skill of the leadership.

Tony entered the wine business in Chicago 60 years ago. His first job was in *his* father's liquor store. Over time he switched to his father-in-law's wine distributorship, also in Chicago.

At that time the U.S. wine market was almost totally commoditized. Distributors bought wine in bulk and simply poured it into new one-gallon bottles. The bottles sold for just $.15-$.25 per gallon. The wines were barely distinguishable one from the other.

That was fine because Americans had neither the desire nor the skill to distinguish between wines. Their only interest was price. If two distributors were selling wine for $.19 per gallon and one dropped his price to $.18 per gallon, he might well capture the market and drive the competitor out of business. But that didn't happen. Why? If a distributor reduced his price by one cent per gallon, he would probably eliminate his profit margin, making the one-cent drop in price the equivalent of a suicide mission. And these wine distributors were anything but suicidal. Like others, the Terlatos were immigrants who had become capitalists. They struggled to support their families and wouldn't do anything that threatened the business that fed them.

When Tony first entered the business, he became a serious student of the wine market. He saw that a small part of the market was *not* commoditized. A Beyond-the-Eaves Vision revealed that imported wines sold for more. For example, while a gallon of bulk wine was selling for $.19 per gallon, a bottle of Château Lafitte Rothschild sold for $3.98 for a fifth of a gallon. (That bottle sells for an incredible $1,500 today.) Tony wanted to know what made some wine sell for so much more than others. So even while at his father's store, Tony worked hard to gain an appreciation of fine wines.

Now, to many people, Tony's hard work would sound like a joyful hobby. He did a lot of wine tasting. Many people do a lot of wine drinking, but that was far from what Tony was about. Tony would bring home different wines, and his wife, Jojo, would pour a glass from each bottle—hiding the bottles from Tony so he could make blind test comparisons.

Of course to do that, Tony had to know what elements to compare. Simultaneously, he had started reading about wines. He read about using your palate to sense that wines *breathe* differently. He worked at it relentlessly for three years, trying to learn from a wine's *legs* ("legs" are streaks that trickle down the side of a wine glass when one swirls the glass before tasting it. "Good legs" indicates higher alcohol or sugar content) and *aroma*, until one night "I really could tell the difference. I really saw simplicity and complexity. I finally recognized the aroma in the simplicity of pasteurized wine." [Terlato #1]

In a dramatic departure from the custom back then, Tony began running tasting demonstrations in his family's store. Customers and even newspaper reporters came on Saturdays, knowing that's when wine-tasting lessons would be taught by Tony.

Still Tony's audience was tiny, and the U.S. market for quality wines was, well, less than significant. That's when Tony's vision was formed, even though he lived in the midst of a country that had no interest in quality wines.

Since wines were picked on price alone, a penny difference ruled. Yet, Tony had a vision: Americans caring about wine quality and selecting their wines accordingly. It wasn't a wild-eyed vision. Tony saw a linkage between fine food and fine wine. He reasoned that Americans cared about food and would, some day, seek gourmet quality food.

When they did, they would gravitate toward higher quality wines. In other words, Tony had both Beyond-the-Eaves and Trend Pattern Vision: he saw what Europe had done regarding pairing food and wine and visualized similar conditions in the United States.

Amazingly, that was in the 1950s. This was an outlandish vision for that time in the U. S. This was when McDonald's first opened—hardly a sign that Americans were leaning toward quality dining. [Terlato #2]

Trend Pattern Vision for Tony was somewhat time-challenged. The revolution he predicted in the 1950s turned out to be an evolution. Son Bill recalls that even by the early 1980s, when he entered the business, "three brands of wine were on every wine list in Chicago: Lancers, Mateus and Blue Nun. They were huge brands. Peoples' taste had matured by the late 1990s. Those three brands had nearly disappeared." The fulfillment of Tony's vision took decades longer than anticipated. But in a centuries-old industry, where aging is a virtue, decades don't matter as much as elsewhere. Tony was prescient to say the least.

Having a vision sounds somewhat passive. One pictures someone sitting and waiting for the proverbial light bulb to illuminate over his or her head. In fact, visionaries generally are a product of others' experiences in other fields or businesses that they observe or read about. For example, Tony Terlato observed what was going on in Europe: Even across the ocean, jug or table wines still served certain needs and markets.

But finer quality bottles of wine were selected for dinners and special occasions. In Europe, those wines represented a much larger share of the market than in the U.S. He observed the relationship of food culture and wine quality. Years of reading books by European wine experts, of observing European society and comparing American society, and of learning (self-taught) how to distinguish and evaluate good wines, had been hard, disciplined work. It was hardly a passive occurrence.

Even after Tony had the vision of Americans caring about the quality of their wine, he did not sit back awaiting its occurrence. He became an active advocate.

▶ He would search for new brands in Europe, and sometimes, in order to get exclusive distribution rights, he would take great risks—sometimes bet-the-company risks—buying quantities the producers demanded, without any assurances that he could sell these high quality wines to his customers.

▶ He would visit his restaurant customers. He'd buy several bottles of their wine, some he had just sold to the restaurateur and others wine from his competition. He would conduct tastings and teach the restaurant proprietors and waiters how to "know" the wines.

▶ He created descriptive wine lists and gave them to his restaurant customers. Then he'd teach the proprietors and waiters how to sell the wines using his wine lists as both teaching materials and sales tools.

By the 1970s, fine European dining was being introduced in the U.S. In Chicago, restaurateurs like Jean Banchet and Jovan Trbojevic were making a mark. Tony befriended Jovan and worked with him to pair quality wines with Jovan's superb food. [Terlato #3]

And it turns out, quality wine trickles down. As a couple of premier restaurants opened, luring away customers from previously top-rated restaurants, those losing out had to upgrade both food and wine to defend their turf. And so on down the quality spectrum. It took a lot of Tony's time and attention. He was the key element in helping the trickling take place. Tony's vision, now reality, was anything but a passive revelation. Nor were Tony's efforts aimed solely at his customers. European suppliers were dubious at best. Their opinions of American's tastes were less than complimentary. They were concerned over selling their wine to an American distributor who might discount prices or otherwise damage their brand.

At first, Tony was lumped into the object of their concern. But Tony knew quality wine, and his knowledge was becoming respected by vintners and bottlers. Vittorio Gancia was a prominent winemaker in Italy. When considering whether to allow Terlato to distribute one of his brands, Gancia asked Tony pointed questions: "How do you perceive this business? Do you want to sell a lot of wine or do you want to sell wine that's very good? What do you want from me?"

Gancia knew a lot about Tony. He had visited the family's stores, and he had dined at home with the Terlato family. He'd had many conversations with Tony about the wine business. No doubt, he was favorably impressed by Tony's answers to the Gancia question: "I want you to make the best Spumante possible. That's what you can do for me."

Still, he remained skeptical of Tony's ability to convert American tastes and habits and his ability to sell more expensive quality wines in the U.S. Here, Tony proved an adept salesman. He was able to sell European wine people on his vision, despite their entrenched negative opinion about Americans' lack of sophistication when it came to the "finer things in life."

He did so by articulating his dream in compelling fashion: Tony put his money, energy and soul where his mouth was.

Terlato: A Family Thing

Tony also wished to keep the company in the family. He wanted his sons and grandchildren to inherit the business. So he started early. Tony hosted other world-famous wine people at dinners in his home and had sons Bill and John attend. (John's interests were directed elsewhere then. But he is now an integral part of the company.) Tony's efforts were primarily aimed at Bill, teaching him to develop an expert palate and to understand the business and every segment of the industry. Tony also instilled his vision, and today Bill has fully adopted his father's vision. Indeed as CEO, Bill now owns his dad's vision of Americans drinking fine quality wine. However, there is a difference between owning a vision and having a vision. [Terlato #4]

Excellence Is the Surest Way to Success

Most visionary business leaders see unique ways of capturing market share, of wresting share from existing players through better pricing (Cosco), better quality (Apple), better service (Amazon), or better business models, such as freemium retailers.

Freemium is a pricing strategy by which a basic product or service—typically a digital offering or application such as software, media, games or web services—is provided free of charge. However, money—a premium—is charged for more valuable proprietary features.

All of these are challenging. All are adaptations of the famous business school study model of a three-legged stool, where one leg stands for service, a second leg stands for pricing, and the third stands for quality. This idea originated in the mind of the late Peter Drucker, world famed management guru.

Often the leader must be more creative and efficient. Sometimes, the leader can take advantage of existing players' flaws or failings, typically arrogance or intransigence, leading to a lack of recognition of the basic principle: "eat your lunch before someone else does."

When someone with an improved product price, service or quality eats your lunch, that business rival takes market share from you while you dither. Since your old or lesser product or service will lose out to the newer, better replacement in any event, it might as well be you and not a competitor whose replacement prevails.

On rare occasions, a business leader envisions something more than stealing a share of an existing market. Such a leader might envision a new market for existing products. That's what occurred with Tony Terlato. With Beyond-the-Eaves and Trend Pattern Visions, he anticipated a huge new market: Americans drinking quality wines just like Europeans were doing.

By the time Bill had assumed the helm as CEO, with dad Tony 'moving upstairs' as chairman, their world had changed. A significant number of Americans were paying attention to the quality of their food and wine. And the number was growing. More and more Americans were developing a taste for better wines. No longer content to drink indistinguishable wines, they learned what they liked, they learned about pairing wines and food, they learned how to select and how to store wines. Few built wine cellars, but sales of small refrigerated wine cabinets definitely increased. Some people bought pocket-sized devices and later apps for their smart phones to guide wine selection. People vacationed in wine locales—the Napa Valley in California, Tuscany, Italy, Champagne, France, Cape Town, South Africa, and Mendoza in Argentina. They shipped home cases of quality wine that they had tasted and bought at discount prices straight from the vineyard.

When that supply was consumed, they frequently ordered more, but this time at local stores' full price and over the internet.

Like any good salesman, Bill was focused on building market share. However, Terlato had already captured a substantial share of the market for wine selling at over $15 a bottle. (Today, Terlato's wines at those prices account for 11% of the total, the largest percentage share of that market.) There is always more share to wrest away, but that wasn't Bill's primary concern.

Forest & Trees Vision told Bill that in addition to his everyday goal of increasing share, there was a macro threat that needed his attention. Trend Pattern Vision told him that the threat was approaching quickly. The looming challenges Bill saw in the future were challenges that Terlato was ill-equipped to handle. To address the imminent challenge, he needed to develop a vision that was totally different than and indeed in conflict with his father's.

Visions May Endure But Not Always As Visions

We have noted that business visions have expiration dates. Unfortunately, the expiration date for a vision is generally invisible.

So where do business visions go when they expire? They may fade as a vision but remain as a company's policy or even a model, in support of or coincidental with a new vision for the business.

Tony Terlato's vision—that Americans would learn to appreciate and pay for quality wines—was revolutionary when he first had his "aha" moment decades earlier. That will forever be his vision, no matter how many years pass. But like packaged turkey slices, there is a "sell by" date. The "sell by" date of a vision like Tony's or anybody else's is invisible.

Thus, Tony's vision, the basis upon which he built a great company, is a relic today, an historical fact. It endures, just not as a vision. Visions are of the future. Tony's vision is now an existing fact, no longer an aspiration. Today, it serves as the basis for existing policy: That they sell only quality wines, no undistinguished table wines.

That doesn't mean that Terlato Wines now lacks a vision. There are many reasons why Tony was willing to step back and make son Bill the CEO. Most important reason: He was ready to lead the company into the future. Over a dozen years of hard work by Tony and Bill, had converted the kid who visited the office and sat in at dinner meetings into the company's leader.

His network, his skills, his knowledge of the product and industry were greater than were Tony's when his dad became CEO. Of course that was facilitated by Bill having Tony's shoulders to stand on. In addition, Bill had a critical prerequisite for taking charge. Like his dad, he had a "vision and capability to lead."

Just as Bill replaced Tony as CEO, so did Bill's vision supplant Tony's vision. It would have been easy for Bill to rest on the laurels Tony's vision had created. Building market share would seem easy—easier than creating it from scratch. Going from 0 to 10 in 40 years is much harder than increasing from 10 at 10% per year, at least up to a point.

Terlato's share could still grow, and if Bill had set out to grow share, who could have complained? On such performance, the Terlato family could ride into a distant sunset. But then Bill had a new vision. To preserve their progress meant creating and controlling their own destiny. Trend Pattern Vision caused Bill serious concern that the horizon loomed far too close.

Tony's vision was based on influencing the *demand* side of the equation. Bill worried that his father's vision, albeit a game changer in its day, was vulnerable on the *supply* side.

As a distributor, Terlato was only as good as its relationships with suppliers. The vendors who were above stream could decide to raise prices, sacrifice quality to increase revenue, go with a different distributor, become or acquire a distributor.

A few such changes could be devastating. Bill's sense of the future made him want control at every level, even owning the vineyards.

He wanted total vertical integration, to assure quality, to prevent interference and, most important, to provide the basis for assuring continuity as a family business. Following that vision would risk all they had achieved. [Terlato #5]

It proved worthwhile rather quickly. Terlato recently lost the exclusive rights to Santa Margherita Pinot Grigio, their biggest product line and almost one-third of their revenue. Taking the vertical integration risk proved prescient. Had they not done so, the loss of Santa Margherita could have been quite impactful. Now having followed Bill's vision, they are doing better than ever.

Note that Beyond-the-Eaves Vision not only entailed observing the actions of competitors but also Bill's own vertical chain—growers, vendors, distributors and retailers.

THE VISION THING

Vintages Notwithstanding, Businesses Periodically Require New Visions

Bill had learned at the feet of his father, and both were excellent salesmen and knew how to meet customers' needs. But some things are beyond the salesman's control.

Bill's vision reflected the fear that Terlato Wines was vulnerable: Were the vineyard owners to sacrifice quality for short term financial benefit or were they to sell to others? In such scenarios, Terlato could be adversely affected. And the only way he could control such critical factors was by controlling what was above stream.

To Bill the vision was clear: Terlato must become a vineyard owner, a bottler and a brand owner.

Today, though Terlato distributes nearly 80 wine brands and about 20 other spirits in the U.S., Terlato Wines also owns or has interests in 10 vineyards. More than this, Terlato Wines owns 11 wine brands or wineries.

Clearly Bill's vision has proved every bit as prescient as his father's. Tony's vision was right for his time and established the company's value. A new vision serves Bill's times well by preserving value. Of course, re-visioning isn't over at Terlato Wines. Bill's daughter and son are already in the business.

Needless to say, implementing Bill's vision necessitated assumption of big risks and flawless operations. Tony's vision also entailed big risks and near perfect operations. But that's where the visions' similarity ends. Like many family businesses, each generation must update goals and aspirations. Sometimes run room remains within the prior generation's vision.

Run room in this case reflects a reasonable interval during which Tony's vision can be expected to provide a reasonable return on investment. Sometimes there is no run room: In those cases, the need for the successor to have a new vision is critical.

Knowing that the successor needs a new vision despite apparent run room, depends on the quality of the successor's new vision *and* the company's ability to implement that vision.

Here's a downer: Occasionally, respect for a parent's vision or fear of parent outrage prevents a timely change of vision.

VISION CHART

(For chapter 4)

▸ A first generation visionary may aim at totally reinventing the marketplace: by raising the level of wine appreciation among consumers. But such an endeavor may require the second generation visionary to totally reinvent the supply system.

▸ Vision collision can destroy a company.

▸ A company's new vision doesn't negate the value of an earlier or first vision, so long as you respect the value of the earlier vision in bringing the company to the point of needing an updated vision.

The Vision Transition

Failure to have a timely re-vision is a major factor in a frightening statistic: 90 percent of family businesses fail to make it through the third generation.

That statistic is not as bleak as it seems. Early action can improve the survival odds markedly.

Tony worked hard to teach his son the business. He explained his vision to Bill but didn't insist that he adopt it. He immersed Bill in his business world but made it a safe atmosphere for Bill to develop his own vision. Bill did that.

You will see that Kay Koplovitz's parental training was hardly typical for a future entrepreneur or for a young girl at that time. Kay's father was not in a business that appealed to her. Her father opted for a less comfortable route. He allowed Kay extraordinary leeway. In many ways he created an atmosphere that enabled Kay to become a visionary with accomplishments anyone would envy.

CHAPTER 5

Kay Koplovitz

Kay Koplovitz:
A Runaway Success

▼▼▼▼▼▼▼▼▼▼▼▼

W hen Kay Koplovitz was 3 years old, she ran away to a nearby kindergarten in her hometown of Milwaukee, Wisconsin. Fiercely independent, she got what she wanted. But when the family moved, and she could no longer walk to Mrs. Water's kindergarten classes, her dad said flatly: "You're going with us!" Then five, she said, "Okay, but you'll have to raise my allowance to 50 cents so I can take the bus to Mrs. Water's class." Advantage Kay. In college she worked at a TV station. In the '60s she knew TV would dominate the means by which the world connected. Back then, top TV execs were delighted just to dominate local markets. She was the first to televise baseball to the world market. When outraged Commissioner Bowie Kuhn warned that her first world telecast of the Yankees was her last, this seasoned-since-five negotiator bested intractable Kuhn with an "Okay," if he'd trade a Major League Baseball contract for her Yankees contract. The lady proved mightier than the lord.

Kay Koplovitz

The Bantam Dynamo Behind
The Thrilla in Manila

Recently, on the occasion of his death, the world feted the life of Mohammed Ali, as likely the greatest boxing champion of all time. There was adulation for the professional boxer as a man of principle, a man willing to sacrifice his coveted title as "Heavyweight Champion of The World," by claiming conscientious objector status and refusing to serve in the U.S. military during the Vietnam War. In addition to being stripped of his title and incurring the wrath of his fans and fellow citizens, he was effectively denied the right to compete as a boxer in the United States of America. To put it bluntly, his career was officially over.

That caused an interesting set of national paradoxes. In the mid-70s, the nation as a whole was not behind the war and lacked appropriate patriotic support of its troops.

Yet the citizenry had sufficient patriotic fervor to denigrate Ali for his decision. Would the loquacious Ali never again float like a butterfly and sting like a bee in the U. S.? So it seemed.

Clever boxing promoters, sensing a pent-up demand for Ali's enormous talent, arranged for him to fight outside the U.S. One such venue was Manila in the Philippines. But boxing fans there and in other such venues were small in number. An even smaller number had the discretionary income to pay big ticket prices for boxing matches. The cost of moving the entourage abroad was huge.

Ali stated that he was "the greatest" and eventually most sports fans were to agree with this outsized self-assessment.

But would Mohammed Ali have been so if his greatness had been kept secret – if no one got to see the bout in Manila?

We'll never know, because the clever promoters, seeking ways to increase the revenue stream, were to put an Ali event on the world map. They struck a deal to televise the event. They called it, "The Thrilla in Manila." That would bring in the immense revenues needed to pay the expense of staging it in the island nation. As for the former World Champion, it gave the public access to his greatness and caused them to appreciate Ali.

This sounds simple, and today it would be. In the mid-1970s, however, it not only wasn't simple but simply impossible. When the event finally occurred, the public believed it was all the work of boxing promoter Don King.

Even more loudmouthed and flamboyant than Ali himself, King, whose hair appeared to have been hit by lightning, was indeed a clever promoter. But wait! While King had a serious role in the promotion, the real enabler of "The Thrilla in Manila" was a petite lady from Milwaukee, Wisconsin whose background was as far from King's as her subdued blonde hair was from his electric bouffant.

Her name is Kay Koplovitz. She created the USA Network, the first global television network. Kay was able to see and to meld the science of satellite technology and the art of television programming as no person— man or woman—had done before.

Kay is a rare example of a multifaceted talent. Her experience and expertise in television, cable television and satellite technology, specifically geosynchronous orbiting satellites, in the 1970s, was unique to say the least.

Kay had the rare expertise to bring together those variegated technical areas and to view the unique combined perspective that they provided. It's not terribly dissimilar from the phoropter refracting instrument, the device ophthalmologists use. You know, the other-world device with metal circular "goggles" that rest on the bridge of your nose, while the doctor interchanges the lenses over each eye as you try to read the letters on the "Big E Chart," formally known as the "Snellen Chart."

The continually changing lenses on the phoroptor seem random, hit or miss until the right combination works: until your vision is clearest. Of course, the doctor's expertise makes the lens selection more scientific than random. So too, Kay's vision was more scientific than random.

While in college at the University of Wisconsin, Kay held a part-time job producing television shows for WHA-TV, an educational station in Madison. A capable and creative producer, she also began to understand the power and potential of this relatively new medium. It piqued her interest and while most of America sat mesmerized by the "boob tube," Forest & Trees Vision enabled her to handle daily minutia, while envisioning the global image of what television could become.

During a $50 per day tour of London, Kay happened to hear a lecture by Arthur C. Clarke, a science-fiction writer and futurist, on the subject of satellite technology.

His prognostications about the power of geosynchronous orbiting satellites to remain stationary in space sent Kay's mind into orbit.

Almost immediately Kay saw how satellites might free television from the artificial constraints of antennae range. She wanted to be part of, indeed to lead, the transformation. She enrolled at Michigan State University and wrote her master's thesis on the subject.

Her dream was huge. Kay says she had not seen any reason not to dream big. She tied television to satellite transmission which would give TV the wings to go global.

At that time, the 1960s, TV was essentially a local business, developed into networks of local stations by pioneers like Bill Paley (CBS) and David Sarnoff (NBC). Kay's dream was to bypass that: enabling concurrent transmission of a program to every TV set in the world. Talk about "vision collision." This was at a time when experts were saying, "No one will pay to watch TV." [Koplovitz #1] Some were experimenting with the concept of "pay TV," using black boxes installed on top of their TV sets. Kay knew that people would pay for top content. This was also a time when no one would back a woman in such an aggressively innovative concept.

After receiving her master's degree, Kay went job shopping. Fortunately she came upon Bob Rosencrantz, the president of UA-Columbia at Cablevision. [Koplovitz #2] Kay has always been fiercely independent: Even at 3 years old when she ran away to go to kindergarten. Then, just as she finally was actually old enough to attend kindergarten, her parents' move meant she'd have to transfer out of Mrs. Water's class.

"I'm not going to be able to move with you," the five year old told her father, "I have to graduate Mrs. Water's kindergarten class." Her father was stern: "You're moving!" Kay said matter-of-factly, "OK, then you have to raise my allowance. I need $.50 a week to take the bus to Mrs. Water's class." Despite her father's stern warning that she dare not ask her mother for a ride on stormy days during Wisconsin's frigid winters, the deal was struck. Defiant Kay did indeed graduate from Mrs. Water's kindergarten class. [Koplovitz #3]

Dreams only go so far. Ultimately, the tests become whether the dreams are good enough to be doable and whether the dreamer is an entrepreneur who is good enough to make that happen. Kay considers herself an entrepreneur.

She has proved she knows how to make her dreams real. She enjoys "setting the rules of the game in determining my own fate—it seduces me.

"It's the ultimate environment for creativity. I like the blank slate to start off and figure out how to solve this to get to where I want to go. When I come up with something, I'm right….Don't get me wrong: I've made lots of mistakes.

"I guess if you ask people they would say, 'Kay had very strong opinions about what she wanted to get done.' "But they would say that I listened to their arguments and that they had every opportunity to voice opinions they wanted to about what we were doing or a different course." [Koplovitz #4]

Using Trending Pattern Vision, she quickly realized that her idea, pay-to-play television, would absolutely devour programming.

Sports and movies were extremely popular, and HBO had movies covered, so the next deal she did was to license over 125 Madison Square Garden events. While that satisfied her mentor, Bob Rosenkranz, Kay's reaction was, "No, we've got to go out and get the rest of sports." [Koplovitz #5]

Ultimately she did just that, NBA, NHL, the Augusta National Golf Tournament, U.S. Open tennis, soccer, track and field—an annual total of 500 live sporting events.

Licensing content, in her case sporting events, and using advertising to produce revenue was then a new combination. Later, it became commonplace, as did subscription revenue combined with licensed content.

Beyond-the-Eaves Vision and Trending Pattern Vision had shown her the best market, and Forest & Trees Vision convinced her that she could handle big-time sports.

Her network was called "Madison Square Garden Sports," but as Kay expanded, its horizons outgrew the name so she renamed the company, "USA Network."

She attributes that success to her "ability to envision something and then to understand how to put it together."

Her father was not her most powerful negotiating foe.

In 1979, she negotiated a deal with George Steinbrenner. He signed a contract to let her televise the New York Yankees games. The first game, against the Yankees' arch rival the Boston Red Sox went into extra innings. She couldn't have asked for a better series launch.

The very next morning she received a call from Baseball Commissioner Bowie Kuhn: "I see you televised the Yankees game last night."

Kay responded, "Yes, I did. It's great for baseball."

She was very happy; exuberant. Kuhn was less so: "That's not why I'm calling you. I'm calling to tell you that you didn't have the right to televise it."

Kay responded, "Yes I do. I have the signed contract from George Steinbrenner sitting right here on my desk."

Kuhn said, "That's not my point, Mrs. Koplovitz. My point is he didn't have the right to sell it to you."

She asked why but continued trying to talk him into letting her carry the Yankees series. Kuhn, a former partner in the prestigious silk stocking law firm, Willkie Farr & Gallagher, was not having any of that. He told her flatly that he was going to get a temporary restraining order to stop Kay from televising the next Yankees' game.

Kay realized her small company didn't have the finances to take on Major League Baseball in a lawsuit and she told the formidable Kuhn she would call him back. Kay conferred with her lawyer husband, who worked at UA Columbia Cable at the time. He made it clear that she was likely to lose a battle with baseball.

Kay was distraught: she had already sold the program into the cable system. Not only would she be embarrassed, her company could be devastated possibly even destroyed. So she returned to her office and called back Bowie Kuhn, trying, once more, to talk him into allowing her to carry the Yankees' games. She knew she was hitting a wall. So she said to him, out of the blue, "OK, I'll trade you."

That silenced Bowie who finally said "I don't understand what you're talking about. Trade me what?"

Kay said, "I'll trade you my Yankees contract for a contract with Major League Baseball." After extended silence, Bowie Kuhn finally said, "I'll see you in my office tomorrow morning, Mrs. Koplovitz."

And that's how she traded her Yankees contract for a Major League Baseball contract for all major league teams. As Kay said to me, "Not bad for one morning's work." [Koplovitz #6]

Certainly not a bad result at all in one morning. It likely was one of the biggest and most important sports contracts up to then. Kay had negotiated successfully against one of the best negotiators of our time, even though he had all the money and power, and even the law, on his side.

But then Kay had been practicing for this since the age of five, when she negotiated for a $.50 allowance to attend Mrs. Water's kindergarten class. Besides, she had vision. Years later, when her dad was in his 90s, Kay was sitting with him. Despite a little dementia he was still cogent. Kay asked him why he had let her have her way—the allowance and busing her way to kindergarten class when she was five.

He said, "Well, I wanted to bring you up to be independent. I trusted you." It seems Kay's father had a vision relating to his daughter, the world television visionary.

▼▼▼▼▼▼▼▼▼▼▼▼▼▼▼▼▼▼▼▼▼▼▼▼▼▼▼▼▼▼▼▼▼▼▼▼

When the Devil is Not in the Details

Kay's focus is not on details: "I'm actually not a person who has intense concentration on details. That is not for me. I think in broad concepts. I'm much more at home in the unknown. I'd like to explore the unknown. So I think the ability to bring large concepts into focus for myself is natural for me. It's what I feel most comfortable doing."

Her husband, William C. Koplovitz, has said that Kay has extraordinary focus. She does, but it may not be what you think. [Koplovitz #7]

I counsel clients, especially entrepreneurs and students to be careful lest their focus deprives them of the peripheral vision to deal with opportunities and challenges. I call such peripheral vision, "Beyond-the-Eaves Vision."

▲▲▲▲▲▲▲▲▲▲▲▲▲▲▲▲▲▲▲▲▲▲▲▲▲▲▲▲▲▲▲▲▲▲▲▲

Forward Movement Often Moves Backwards

Kay then told me about a meeting she'd had the day before our interview. It was with a man she considered extraordinarily prescient. Turns out, he was dyslexic and was exploring how dyslexia functions in the brain.

Kay continued, "I am a little bit dyslexic. I have attributes of it. I transpose letters. Many people do that."

The man she met with explained that, remarkably, many entrepreneurs, engineers, and artists have dyslexia.

I have been a consultant to and known a number of dyslectic entrepreneurs. Their condition clearly contributed to their ability to see what the rest of us can't see: we hear incomprehensible noises where they see visions.

She went on to explain that this expert has a website with all kinds of documentation, and even has done TED Talks on it. TED Talks are influential videos from expert speakers on education, business, science, tech and creativity.

"He started explaining to me that people with dyslexia have different connections in the brain.

"Brain connections are really like telephone poles that are communicating with one another. In normal people, the poles are very close together. With people that are on the dyslexia spectrum, the [poles] are far apart, which makes it more difficult to concentrate on details. But this makes it enormously possible for them to see a wide spectrum."

As he was describing this to Kay, she thought, "It's so funny, because it really describes my behavior." She went on to say that her dyslexia expert said his studies had shown that an incredible half the NASA scientists are dyslexic.

Could that explain why Kay tied orbiting satellites and television together? In my view, Kay ranks with the rocket scientists.

THE VISION THING
Great Visionaries Can Miss a Beat, Too

Kay did well in business but never realized what I would consider the appropriate financial reward for her amazing creativity and innovation. She was never allowed to own any significant part of the business she developed, not even when it sold in 1998 for $4.5 billion.

What she had in scientific and artistic vision she lacked in financial know-how. On the other hand, these were times when women were arbitrarily excluded from positions of such power.

She felt fortunate to get a job and did not want to jeopardize that opportunity and the means it gave her to exercise her creativity.

She felt that pushing for a piece of the action, which she had been told by her boss and others was not in the cards would mean losing the jobs she valued so highly.

Vision Chart

(For Chapter 5)

▶   Whatever your focus it should be the beginning not the end of your life plan. It should form the basis for blending your multi disciplines, as Kay did by adding satellite know-how to her television experience.

▶   In business, 'no' needn't be the end of the road and can be an invitation to negotiation, as Kay demonstrated with Bowie Kuhn.

▶   When everyone says it will never happen, e.g., "people won't pay to watch TV that's always been free," they simply may not have your vision.

The Vision Transition

Kay's understanding of the then-new media form, television, might have enabled her to have a career in TV. Her educational focus on the science of satellite technology could have enabled her to seek a career in that area. Either could have proved fertile ground for a talent, intellect and drive like Kay's. Combined they afforded an extraordinary opportunity for an amazing talent. The combination gave her a leg up over possible competitors, few if any of whom had such dual capabilities. The effect: The whole was far greater than the sum of the parts. That was an advantage in Kay's generation; it may prove a prerequisite in the future.

Kay Koplovitz's father established an atmosphere of freedom to help her become independent when she was just five. This gave her the confidence to look farther out, to become a visionary. Her experience and education combined to form a galactic corridor large enough to contain her vision.

Ross Perot Sr.'s father allowed Ross to start working at age five, to develop a solid work ethic, and so Ross had a clear understanding of what it was like being an employee. His father's exemplary way of dealing with his employees taught Ross leadership. This and other nurturing factors gave Ross confidence that he could do whatever he could envision, and he passed these lessons on to make a visionary of his son, Ross, Jr.

CHAPTER 6

Ross Perot, Sr. and Ross Perot, Jr.

The Perots: Ross Sr. and Ross Jr. The Apple Seed Flew Far From the Tree

▼▼▼▼▼▼▼▼▼▼▼▼

*T*he Perots seem to sense needs before prospective customers and other stakeholders recognize needs exist. In the operational sense, even as Ross, Sr. was selling to the max of IBM's commission structure, he envisioned IBM's customers wanting something totally different. But after all, who was Ross Perot to tell IBM how to run the business? A generation later, Ross, Jr.'s vision told him that the U.S. needed a port even if land-locked for goods shipped out of neighboring Mexico. More than merely sensing needs, both Perots felt they had what it took to fulfill their visions. Is that confidence? Yes, but not in the way most people think of confidence and certainly not just confidence. Ross Jr. says his father is a visionary from whom he has learned about being a visionary. Their stories reveal important lessons about being a business visionary.

It would be easy to say Ross Perot, Jr. flew a path widely different from that of his famously-successful father. Ross, Sr. who was U.S. Navy through and through (and class president all four years he studied at Annapolis). He would later start a software company which he sold for over $2 billion.

Then he started another which he and Ross, Jr. built and sold for billions more.

Ross had wanted his son to go Navy. But Ross, Jr. chose the Air Force. [Perot #1] Not surprising: He had become the first person to fly a helicopter around the world. With the family's successful sale of the two software companies complete, Ross, Jr. turned his part of the family fortune away from technology. He moved his focus to real estate and used Dallas land he acquired to build the largest landlocked port of entry in the country.

Despite his deep respect for and love of his father, Ross Jr.'s vision conflicted with the early vision of his father. Jr.'s port receives goods made in Mexico. The Mexican goods are a result of the Free-Trade Agreement so strongly opposed by his father, Ross, Sr. During a third party run for president, in 1992, the elder Perot argued that free trade with low-wage Mexico would cause a "giant sucking sound" as high-paying U. S. jobs moved south of the border.

Ross Perot Sr. was industrious almost from his days as a toddler. *His* father was a Texas cotton trader. According to Ross, *his* father "was doing fine in the cotton business, and it's not as though we were desperate for money." But Ross had his first job at age 5, selling Christmas cards, garden seeds and subscriptions to the *Saturday Evening Post.*

By age 7, he was working for the Texarkana Gazette, riding his bicycle around town collecting for unpaid classified ads.

All this because Ross thought working and earning money "would be interesting." He learned a lot from those experiences in the commercial world but mostly he learned from his father.

Here is a man who always led his class at Annapolis where they teach a few things about leadership; a man who led his employees as he started and grew major companies; and a man who ultimately sought to be leader of the free world. Yet he proclaims: "I learned leadership from my dad, not at the Academy. I watched the way he treated all the people who worked for him. He treated people with dignity and respect. He didn't punch people around or push them. He motivated them by the way he treated them. And if they did a good job, he would give them a bonus. [Perot #2]

"Every year, he would take African American employees to the local Bowie County Fair. And this was at a time when, sometimes, Black people were treated rudely.

"But with them being there with my Dad, they all just had a great time, and it was a good experience for him."

Ross was also impressed that, a couple of times a year, his father attended services at his Black employees' church. His father's spirit-of leadership emanated from within by his making himself part of his employees' lives.

Similarly, his dad put himself in customers' shoes. When Ross's father died, news articles referred to his being a great storyteller and salesman—two traits Ross clearly "inherited." [Perot #3]

Ross's first vision was of his father's exemplary behavior. Later, it became a Retro Vision for both Ross Sr. and Ross Jr.

Perot's appointment to the U.S. Naval Academy was neither easy nor automatic. He finally won an appointment to the Academy after two fruitful years preparing at the local junior college.

Perot was not one of Annapolis's early choices. Most of the early choices were well connected. Those admitted late in the game tended to be hesitant. Not Ross Perot. In junior college, Ross had created an annual yearbook. Hearing of that, the Academy's Superintendent asked Ross to create the Academy's first yearbook and the honor system for the academy. Ross was delighted. That required Ross to interact one-on-one with all the members of the class. This became his unofficial route to a successful campaign for class president, the position he held without serious challenge all four years.

After graduation, Ross spent four years at sea, first on a destroyer and then on an aircraft carrier. As assistant navigator he was normally on the bridge giving orders and coordinating complex activities—launching planes and refueling ships.

One of the men visiting the bridge was Stan Farwell, a World War II hero, known as "Fearless Farwell," who by then was an executive vice president of IBM. Farwell told the captain he was impressed with Perot. The captain mentioned that Perot's father had just died and Ross was leaving the Navy to go home and care for his mother.

Farwell offered Ross a job at IBM. Ross's reply: "You're the first person to offer me a job. I'd certainly like to talk with you, but I don't know much about IBM." [Perot #4]

This was in 1957. By then IBM was a 46 year-old company and the giant of its industry. Ross's lack of knowledge about IBM reflected his focus on the Navy, which he loved.

Perot had a strong work ethic. The goal was hard work to cover his needs and for work's sake, not for money as such. He willingly accepted fortune when earned, but he likely would have been satisfied if it never came. Ross did his homework on IBM and joined the sales training program. At the time, IBM had the most sophisticated sales training program in the world.

It's difficult to know for certain just how good those IBM- trained salesman were. For in those days, the people who made decisions to buy computer equipment were often afraid not to buy from IBM. People said: No one ever got fired buying IBM.

Upon completing the training program, Perot was sent out to sell computers. Boy, did he sell computers! Apparently Ross had learned a bit from his early experiences selling cards, seeds and magazine subscriptions. After his first month in 1962, Perot had sold so much that he was told he would not be allowed to sell any more during the remaining eleven months of the year. He had maxed out his year's pay: His commissions for that one month exceeded the IBM limit for a full year. [Perot #5]

▼▼▼▼▼▼▼▼▼▼▼▼▼▼▼▼▼▼▼▼▼▼▼▼▼▼▼▼▼▼

The Paradox of Salesman Incentive Pay

Back then, a number of large companies had similar policies. Ned Heiser, founder of Allstate Insurance's venture capital subsidiary, and Stan Golder, who developed and ran First Chicago Investment Corp, the venture fund for The First National Bank of Chicago, both had similar experiences.

Their departments posted spectacular results. Heiser told me his subsidiary had used only a few percent of Allstate's capital while accounting for nearly half of its income. Golder related that The First National situation was comparable.

Both Ned and Stan knew they couldn't retain their talented staff if they only paid base salaries.

Those staffers knew what they could make elsewhere. They knew they could demand handsome packages based on results.

So Stan and Ned went to their respective CEOs and asked permission to change the compensation packages for their teams to enable them to make much more than their salaries if results justified the additional compensation. (They didn't ask for themselves, only for their teams.)

In both instances, the requests were denied, basically for the same reason. If the compensation formulas were changed to bring them into line with market rates these sales people would make more than the parent companies' CEOs.

That was intolerable to the CEOs. They rejected the proposals, even though they knew the teams would leave. This eventually caused earnings of both companies to drop. That's arrogance!

These departures ultimately resulted in the creation of some of the most successful venture capital and private equity firms in the world, including GTCR, Summit and Madison Dearborn. The net effect was inevitable: Both Allstate and First National missed out on billions of dollars in profits.

▲▲▲▲▲▲▲▲▲▲▲▲▲▲▲▲▲▲▲▲▲▲▲▲▲▲▲▲▲▲

Ever-loyal, Ross tried to explain his observations to IBM: telling them that many customers were less interested in the hardware IBM was selling and preferred to buy the services the IBM computers provided. He suggested that IBM sell customer services by writing software created for individual industries.

IBM rejected that idea. Following Trend Pattern Vision, Ross left to start Electronic Data Systems – EDS. He borrowed the $1,000 he needed to incorporate from his wife, Margot.

This visionary had outwitted IBM, pioneering the technology services industry, now a $350 billion global segment.

The lessons Ross had learned from his father in the cotton store included critical intuitive aspects of leadership: sizing up people, understanding what motivates them and what he could do to help them be better. During his years at Annapolis and in the Navy, he was exposed to officers and enlisted men who were talented, men who were good learners and eager to do well. So when he founded EDS, they were the people he hired.

Ross hired officers who had been trained as systems engineers and enlisted men to work in his computer centers.

Intuitively, Ross applied another plus he learned at the Academy. His college education had been paid for by the U.S. government. So he was quick to assist his new employees in taking advantage of education opportunities under the G.I. Bill. [Perot #6]

That not only gave him smarter systems engineers and computer jockeys, it created devoted employees whose lives he had improved. Loyalty and devotion generally move both ways.

Fearless Farwell wasn't the only big shot Perot met in the Navy. Many Perot classmates became admirals and government officials. Government was growing and in desperate need for help with computers. Doors opened, and Electronic Data Systems became a large vendor to the U.S. Government.

One of EDS's other big government customers was the Shah of Iran. Perot considered Iran to be the only safe place in the Middle East. He was totally shocked when the Shah was overthrown and two of EDS's top men were imprisoned.

This was around the same time as when the U.S. Embassy in Tehran was taken and its personnel held hostage for hundreds of days. Our government did nothing. This was inconsistent with Perot's "get it done" approach. One of his famous quotes: "The activist is not the man who says the river is dirty. The activist is the man who cleans up the river."

The Iran EDS captives were men for whom Perot felt responsible, maybe more so because he had misjudged Iran. In any event, the U. S. military had a rule that no military person is to be left behind. Ross turned to former military people who worked for him, including Colonel Arthur D. ("Bull") Simons, a World War II hero and a founder of the Special Forces.

Perot asked Simons to pick a team from among the EDS staff and go in and free the two EDS prisoners. This wasn't an example of an executive hiding behind his desk while sending his troops into harm's way. Colonel Simons needed someone to give the two prisoners instructions on what to do when Simons led his men to break them out, he turned to Perot. [Perot #7]

He thought Perot was the only one the Ayatollah might give access. So he asked Perot to go to Iran and visit the two men in prison. This was not a safe time for an American to go to Iran. But of course, Perot did go to Iran—a truly brave act. Intuitively, it made sense. But it was gutsy and not likely to be widely imitated by other corporate CEOs. It probably is one of the reasons the employees were so loyal to Perot. They knew he would have their backs, in the truest sense of that phrase.

Before leaving, Perot called his son and said, "If I don't get back, you have to quit school, go home and take care of the family." Clearly Perot understood the risks. Ross Jr. understood his own responsibilities too. He recalled the story of how, when his grandfather died, his father had to quit the Navy, which he loved so much. Likewise, Ross Jr. knew he would have to halt his education and career, because "family comes first."

Perot wasn't through. After returning from Iran, he had to bring a plane to Turkey, go back to Iran to reconnoiter with Simons and then have the plane ready to pick up the men after Perot's private army got them freed. The amazing story was told by Ken Follett, in the book and later the movie, "On the Wings of Eagles." I mention this story here to help describe part of the scope and evidence of Perot's visionary leadership.

EDS thrived. In a few years, it grew to be a successful company. This was, you may recall, three decades before the 'dot com' bubble years, when companies were sold for fortunes just after they were founded. And it was well before companies were routinely being sold for billions of dollars. So when Perot received a call, indicating that General Motors was interested in buying EDS, he paid attention.

GM offered Perot what he refers to as "a huge sum." The sale price was worth $2.5 billion of GM stock, truly a huge sum.

It would make Perot GM's largest shareholder. In addition, Ross was offered a seat on the GM Board of Directors. Loads of money and the prestige of a seat on an iconic board likely was enough to seal the deal. Perot was not one to seek every last dollar. Besides, Perot was already thinking about new customer needs and additional opportunities. However, Roger Smith, the CEO of GM, was a pretty good salesman too. He wasn't taking any chances. He wanted to be sure Perot said yes: "Sell us EDS so you can help turn GM around."

Smith's predecessor, Charlie Wilson had become U.S. Secretary of Defense. In confirmation hearings Wilson famously said "…I thought what was good for our country was good for General Motors and vise versa."

To Perot, Wilson's remark meant he had to do the deal—*so he could turn around GM.* That's because in Perot's mind this was the patriotic thing to do. Besides, he knew he could do the job and assumed that was Smith's thinking too.

The GM acquisition had it all—a huge fortune, prestige and patriotism. To Perot this acquisition seemed like a deal made in heaven. However, the climb was interrupted by a stormy clash of cultures magnified by Perot's patriotic sense and his pursuit of a huge liquidity opportunity. [Perot #8]

▼▼▼▼▼▼▼▼▼▼▼▼▼▼▼▼▼▼▼▼▼▼▼▼▼▼▼▼▼▼▼▼▼

Culture Clash: When a Mighty Force Strikes the Immovable Object

Almost all mergers and acquisitions have culture clashes which good leaders try to resolve. Here, there was more: the respective mindsets of the two men were totally incompatible.

While GM had approached Perot, the super salesman in him had convinced GM that EDS was a perfect company for GM—in the right place and time and with the right product. Shortly after the deal was closed, Ross proposed expanding EDS to provide additional services to customers. His vision was to help GM: to turn it around. Smith was focused on other goals.

Mindful of his mission—turning around GM—Perot did what no other GM director or top executives did: he went down to the factory floors and talked with union employees.

That may have seemed extraordinary for GM's largest shareholder but not for a man who risked his life to help rescue two of his employees in Iran or for the son of a cotton trader who went to church with his African American employees.

In fact, he couldn't believe that GM executives never did so. But why would they? They had no intention of changing things. Besides, being a top exec or director at GM was lucrative, secure, comfortable and even "cushy" as Ross was to describe it. Might you think "it ain't broke, you don't fix it"—if you had a cushy job at the iconic General Motors?

But Perot had read the news reports that described the poor quality of GM cars. The quality comparison was especially stark relative to Japanese cars that were invading the US market.

Hoping to refocus Smith's point of view, a change Perot considered mandatory, he asked Smith what GM was good at?

Smith didn't answer, so Perot asked, "Well, is GM good at anything? Let's set a goal this year to have one product that is the best in the world. I don't care if it's a cigarette lighter. Just try to be the best." Clearly Perot's frustration was escalating. No doubt he was nearing the redoubtable Smith's tolerance level.

Not All Cars Are Created Equal

At that time, one of the perks for GM directors was that they got a new car every three months. Knowing his son would enjoy driving a Corvette, Perot arranged delivery of one, which he and Ross Jr. drove. Both were impressed with what a great car it was. So they were puzzled by the bad press GM car quality drew in the papers. Ross told that to CEO, Roger Smith. Smith replied, "Ross, I have to tell you, the cars that go to directors aren't just off the line. Those cars first undergo special improvements." This insight helped define "cushy" for Ross.

With that in mind, Perot predicted GM would soon go bankrupt. But GM was one of America's venerable companies and one of its most valuable. Clearly Perot was wrong. (In fact, GM was able to hang in there for 25 years before going bust.)

Perot tried to exercise Forest & Trees Vision, visiting the factories and talking with employees while maintaining focus on the "big picture," despite management's attempts to obscure and control his vision by providing doctored cars to directors. Big picture action proposed by Smith also made no sense to Perot.

In 1984, GM was considering acquiring Hughes Aircraft. Ross did his due diligence and then told Smith it made no sense for GM to go into the aircraft business. A GM director, valuing his cushy position, just didn't vote against management proposals. Not even if he was Ross Perot—GM's largest shareholder. However, Ross *did* vote against the Hughes deal, probably being the first to vote against management in a long time. Result: Roger told him he had to leave. But for that to happen, GM had to buy back all of Perot's GM stock.

Knowing that, Perot calculated a "crazy" buy-back price. It clearly included a sizable premium over an already "huge price." But Perot was frustrated and mad. Ross, Jr. says his dad didn't expect Smith to accept the price demand. So Perot was shocked that Smith immediately agreed to Perot's admittedly aggressive request. The payout premium: $750 million. Ross considered the payment wrong and escrowed the money to give the General Motors Board the opportunity to come to their senses and retract it.

Obviously, money does matter. It provides the means for pursuing one's vision. But the vision also matters, and Perot had a vision, a Trend Pattern Vision that showed him how customers wanted more than EDS was offering. If EDS was reluctant to adopt Ross's vision, he had no reluctance. So Perot had asked for—and got—even more. GM would allow him to select 200 GM/EDS guys to help him start a new company. The only stipulations: Perot couldn't start the company for 18 months.

What's more, the new venture couldn't be profitable for the first 18 months after that. A start-up with no profits for 18 months? This was no hurdle for a start-up. Not even one begun by Ross Perot. It is an extraordinarily rare start up that prints black ink on the bottom line that soon. [Perot #9]

U. S. Postal Service: The Big One That Got Away

Once again, Perot was at the juncture of industry and government. Both were missing opportunities that the Perots could help them achieve—if they partnered with Perot.

This is not so different from EDS helping government improve its capacity to use its computers effectively. Nor was it unlike future efforts by Ross and his son.

There was one opportunity for a similar game plan that eluded Perot, through no fault of his own. After his separation from GM, Perot, Sr.'s new company, Perot Systems secured a large contract with the U.S. Post Office. GM sued Perot alleging violations of their contract with him. The suit proved frivolous, but its mere filing scared away the post office. Perot's vision—his intuition was filled with confidence that Perot Systems could fix the post office, and the Post Office doors opened easily based on Perot's reputation, only to be thwarted by GM's anger, big war chest and considerable influence.

Just cooling his heels wouldn't have fit Perot's personality and character. He used the time to prepare: to select and sign up good people and to plot his game plan. That didn't quite fully occupy Perot, so, once again, he started to dabble in real estate and energy. This wasn't the first time Perot had invested in real estate and energy; after all, he was a Texan. When EDS was running smoothly, before the sale to GM, Perot worked on building both his real estate and oil and gas businesses. For Perot, boredom wasn't just distasteful, it was intolerable.

Precisely 18 months after severing his GM ties, he started Perot Systems. Trend Pattern Vision told him how the industry was progressing. Beyond-the-Eaves Vision inspired him to provide software services to bring entire industries into an era in which computers handled data processing at warp speed.

During the period of EDS's growth, Perot's family was also growing, rounding out at seven. He, and wife Margot, married 60 years, have four daughters and his son, Ross Jr.

▸▲▲▲▲▲▲▲▲▲▲▲▲▲▲▲▲▲▲▲▲▲▲▲▲▲▲▲▲▲▲▲◂

Ross Perot, Jr.: Les Petit Prince? Non!

Perot's first child, Ross Jr., was born in 1958. Like many first-borns, he assumed the role of the little prince. He was often reminded, as part of family lore, that immediately after his birth, his grandmother moved to Fort Worth just to be with her new first grandson. The emotional coronation was short-lived. Early on, like his father, he sought jobs to earn money.

At the time of Ross, Jr.'s birth, his dad was a new IBM hiree and Margot was a schoolteacher. But by the time Ross Jr. was ten years old, the situation had changed. EDS went public and created a media-frenzy. One article was entitled, "Fastest, Richest Texan Ever." Really? If not, it would be hard to pinpoint a fitting rival.

Ross Jr. remembers his father calling together the family: "Look, 'Fortune Magazine' is about to do an article on me. It's going to be about the money we've made. It's not important. Don't pay attention to it and just go on about your life." Perot and his wife always worked at making the kids feel normal.

Well it wasn't *just* "an article." It was the feature article, with Perot's picture on the cover. Next day, Ross Jr.'s teacher and friends commented on the article. So much for normalcy! [Perot #10]

Yet his parents' efforts seem to have worked. Ross Jr. mowed the family's lawn to make money. Why? His father wouldn't just give him money.

When business success enabled the Perots to move into a much bigger house with a significantly larger lawn, Perot replaced Ross Jr. with a landscaping company. That caused Ross Jr. to garden for neighbors. This hadn't cooled his ardor for making money. Other "business ventures" followed.

Ross Jr. also made money trading horses for a time. At the age of 16, Ross Jr. bought a horse for $5,000. Not too long after that, an interested buyer offered $15,000 for the horse, to which Ross Jr. countered at $20,000. The buyer was not interested at the higher price. One week later, the horse died.

His dad was a tough negotiator, with seemingly extraordinary intuition. But Ross Sr. also did his homework and had great trading instincts. When he negotiated hard, he generally knew he was in a position to succeed.

Having said that, the older Perot's intuition and vision were by no means infallible. In the 1970s, Perot Sr. was given the opportunity to buy substantial interests in Microsoft, Apple, and Home Depot, all at low cost. But he chose not to do so.

(He also had an opportunity and agreed to buy a substantial piece of Fed Ex when early institutional investors declined to participate in a subsequent financing round. When Fred Smith told his shareholders of Perot's willingness, they were suddenly willing to buy up the round, and no stock remained for Perot.)

Ross, Jr., much like his father before him, avidly sought out money-making opportunities early on. In college, he parked cars one night a week. And in fact, while still in college, his entrepreneurial skills bloomed: He started a shirt company.

He pitched then-unknown Ralph Lauren, because he believed Lauren's Polo brand would succeed—an early sign of Ross, Jr.'s business visionary capability. He secured the franchise to sell Polo products on two college campuses.

Unexpectedly, Polo was late delivering inventory. This delay stuck Ross with out-of-season goods. Undaunted, he ran free beer parties. Unlimited beer made the attendees sufficiently receptive to buy off-season shirts and use their parents' credit cards to pay. [Perot #11]

When Ross Jr. was home from college, he spent his Saturdays at the office with his father. One day, Ross asked his father what would happen if they lost all their money. His dad replied without a pause and showing no dismay that they'd start over, shining shoes and work their way back. [Perot #12]

Ross Perot, Sr. and His North Dallas Vision

Ross Perot had dabbled in raw land in the 1970s. Sunday had traditional observances: church, lunch and a drive in his Lincoln to North Dallas and the farm site Perot owned there.

Sitting in the car, he'd wax eloquent in describing his vision for the property: "There are going to be office buildings, homes and shopping centers…."

The Perot kids loved their father and had confidence in him but, as Ross Jr. put it: "We'd be in the backseat rolling our eyes." He went on to say that today, the property reflects their father's vision and "is a major part of greater Dallas." Needless to say the kids were in awe of dad's vision for the raw land, a vision they once thought overblown.

Ross didn't have a crystal ball. It wasn't that he could touch raw land with a divining rod and see the future.

He did, however, have great Beyond-the-Eaves and Trend Pattern Vision. He could see the cities, Dallas and Fort Worth, creeping beyond their borders. Once he could envision that, he could push the first domino, filling in the areas properly with the obvious needs: commercial and industrial operations create new jobs that create needs for homes, which create needs for stores, and so on.

The Sweet Sorrow Of A Visionary Parting

By the time Ross Jr. came home from college, his father was doing extraordinarily well. The previous year, Forbes had come out with a list of the wealthiest Americans, featuring Walmart's Sam Walton of Arkansas as #1 and Ross Perot of Texas as #2, building stature for the Perots' Texarkana border region.

Perot wanted his son to join him in business. He saw Ross Jr. as smart, capable and a sponge when it came to learning about business. And he wanted to spend more time with his son.

Given Perot's taxing business schedule, it seemed the only way to manage this was for the two to be in business together.

Ross Jr. grew up with early EDS team meetings taking place at the Perot kitchen table. But he was not a computer guy at heart.

In family businesses, a parent needs to be a visionary about family members. Perot realized his son was focused on real estate. Once again, his dad was delighted to show him the way.

Vision II: Plano, Texas

Ross Jr.'s college graduation gift was flying lessons. He would fly over his Dad's 2,500 acre ranch, which became a project called "Legacy." Perot would tell Ross Jr., "Someday this will be downtown Plano." And so it is: Today it's inhabited by Toyota, J C Penney, Frito-Lay, and Hewlett-Packard.

Along the way, Ross Jr. grew to love real estate. Seeing that, Perot told him, "If you like real estate, jump into it." So in 1981, he borrowed money from his dad and bought 100 acres, rezoned it and sold it in 18 months. He doubled his money.

Afterward, he repaid his Dad and reinvested the balance. He then repeated the process two more times, but less favorably: the market had begun correcting. Ross Jr. had his first lesson in cyclicality. [Perot #13] Intuitively, he switched over to Perot oil and gas businesses. The Texas economy—so strong in the 1970s and early 1980s—slid with the deep recession of 1982. Matters really came apart in Texas when oil prices dropped in the mid-1980s. There too, the boom quickly turned to bust. The Perot exposure was limited because they had no debt. Others were highly leveraged. Those fared poorly, many going bankrupt.

Dallas Loses a Jewel in its Economic Crown

Around that time, Braniff Airways went under. Braniff was a major airline, with a big presence in its headquarters, Dallas. Braniff executives were close to the Perots.

Ross Jr. said, "We thought Braniff could never fail. It was a very marked lesson for me." They had provided planes for the Perot rescue in Iran, as well as for a previous exploit when Perot had rescued U.S. servicemen captured by North Viet Nam.

So Perot Sr. told his son to go to the airport, walk through the terminals, and see what bankruptcy looks like. He told his son to be sure to think about the people who had lost their jobs. [Perot #14]

Ross Perot, Jr.: Learning at the Master's Elbow

Ross Jr. talks about the many lessons he learned from his father—lessons about business, faith, family, and about life. He talks about learning optimism, timing, courage, belief and even about how to be a visionary.

To that list I'd add how to judge and motivate people. Perot didn't tell his son to walk the airport terminal to see the wasted assets. He told his to think about the people who lost their jobs.

The Perots had great vision, the foundation for businesses scaled larger than they could run alone. So they learned how to hire people who would do that well. The Perots' job was made easier by confidence in their employees: selected based on their backgrounds, such as military service, and trained in the Perot organizations to be better than they would have been otherwise.

That confidence and trust enabled the Perots to step back and let those people do their thing. Proof that those visions passed to Ross Jr. is found in his instructions to his employees: "Do whatever you think best, do whatever you want, unless you need money. Then come to me."

Ross Jr. had interrupted his development as a businessman in 1982 to make the first helicopter flight around the world. He then served in the Air Force briefly and returned home as a reservist to resume his career as a business innovator. [Perot #15]

That's when Ross Jr. got more involved in real estate. The real estate industry is generally known for its cyclicality, but at that time probably nowhere as much as in Texas. Many oil and gas speculators became momentary land Titans but most of them were to sink like the Titanic. Drive across Texas and you will ride over a seemingly limitless quantity of land. The Texas-sized acreage numbers were subject to extreme high and low prices.

The Perots invested in real estate limited partnerships. But when the tax laws changed, many Perot partnerships went bust. While working out the bankruptcies the message here was reinforced when Ross, Jr. walked the empty Braniff terminal.

The turmoil was exacerbated when the Savings and Loan industry bubble burst. This led to the worst bank crisis since the 1930s. The government established the Resolution Trust Corporation (RTC) and rescued savers under the Federal Savings & Loan Insurance Corporation. In the process, hundreds of the "thrifts" were to fail or were merged and saved at an incalculable cost to the nation's taxpayers.

The first phase of the taxpayer bailout cost $123 billion. The second phase was thought to run three times as high.

Turmoil can generate opportunities to buy land at steeply reduced prices. Ross Jr. told me, "Some real estate investors were actually tripling their money in 24-hour periods."

Ross Jr. took advantage of the opportunities, buying land from the RTC. In fact, 19,000 acres bought then became Ross Jr.'s, Hillwood/Alliance port project. But unlike other investors, many of them really smart, he wasn't chasing the land bubble.

His father had taught him to focus on underlying values, saving him from a blind-guess type of intuition. When father told son: "Never short Texas and certainly don't short America," it wasn't blind patriotism but a practiced perception—a vision—along with a broad understanding of the situation.

Texas land values regressed in the turmoil of the late 1980s to levels of the 1960s. The Perots were big buyers. In addition, Ross Jr. played a form of real estate arbitrage: He sold land in Dallas while buying land in nearby Fort Worth. This strategy reflected unique market disparities. Sellers who succumbed to general economic or real estate conditions were blinded to local real estate values. Fort Worth property was near the Dallas Fort Worth Airport. With this plus it had an edge at the time. That ability to focus on local factors as exceptions to the macro factors—which were the focus of others—was rare indeed. Beyond-the-Eaves Vision needn't be far beyond the eaves.

The Lonely, Uncertain Path of the Contrarian

Beyond-the-Eaves Vision and Trend Pattern Vision, like all the forms of visions I describe, while helpful tools are not silver bullets. Each vision can be applied to different locations and time frames. Where many viewed local trends and techniques, Perot envisioned both remote and local trends and events. When others were blinded by the fog accompanying recessions, Perot saw through the fog to the safe landing pad beyond.

Most importantly, EDS and the sale to GM gave the Perots enormous liquidity, where others had none. This enabled Ross Jr. to benefit from opportunities that others could not avail themselves of. On the other hand, Ross Jr. explained that they "bent over backwards" not to take advantage of other players.

Indeed, in many cases the Perots helped neighbors and competitors. The appreciation that resulted brought long-term relationships and loyalties that proved invaluable for years.

Ross Jr. says "We are more instinct players than analytical investors." Of course, the Perots also have solid analytical people on hand: "But my father is a great visionary. Growing up with a visionary, watching fields become downtowns, you start to pick up the vision. You learn to be a visionary. [Perot #16] You believe. "You learn optimism. You learn timing. You learn that it's great to be contrarian, but that to do so, you must have courage. The mark of a true contrarian is that you're buying when no one else is out there buying. It's cold and it's lonely." [Perot #17]

Readers will recall that Baron Rothschild of the legendary Rothschild banking family was reputed to say: "Buy when there's blood in the streets." It takes courage to emulate such contrarianism. But in truth it takes more. Being a visionary does not spread by mere osmosis. What Ross Jr. learned from his Dad was how to step back and see the big picture or when necessary, how to focus on local factors when others are blinded by the big picture; how to gauge the different aspects of a situation; and how to determine what was and what was not in their sphere of knowledge and influence. That leads to an understanding: what legacy could be more valuable than Beyond-the-Eaves, Trend Pattern and Forest & Trees Visions?

Is Altruism Dead in a World Dominated by Greed?

Ross Perot, Sr. developed the infrastructure for his brand of visionary early in life. As a result of parental, church and community influences and his own personality, he enjoyed working to earn money. He developed an understanding of and expertise at reading and leading people. He also became a devoted patriot. It's important to note that Perot's strong desire to earn money did not encompass *particular* money goals. He found satisfaction working for the Navy. The Navy is not known for its high compensation. He even talked about returning to the Navy if his businesses failed. Indeed, as a boy he worked hard to earn merit badges. He did that so well that he became an Eagle Scout in just thirteen months. Productivity for its own sake is a lost art for many. This is a difficult concept for an all-too-greedy society to comprehend. It was an integral part of his visionary background.

His work ethic wasn't clouded by greed. He willingly accepted money earned but offered to return it if he considered it wrong. And work for work's sake or to achieve noble goals was the guiding light for his visions.

The Great Recession

In 2008 over-heating of financial markets precipitated the severe economic meltdown. Ross Jr. scrambled to adjust holdings to reflect the new circumstances. The markets in which the Perots were invested—oil, gas and real estate—were in turmoil. Ross Jr. was by then even more adept at coping with—and indeed thriving—during recurring cycles.

"It is almost biblical" he said, recalling the Egyptian Pharaoh who turned to a slave named Joseph for help. Joseph interpreted Pharoah's dreams of fat cows followed by emaciated cows to mean seven years of plenty would lead inexorably to seven years of famine. [Perot #18] During the summer of 2008, when fossil fuel prices were soaring, Ross Jr. sold the large Perot inventory of natural gas. That was based on his appraisal of fluctuating underlying values, one of the early visionary lessons he learned from his dad. Oil was still $100 a barrel.

Then the price of oil collapsed. Since the Perots were liquid with proceeds from EDS and GM, they were able to help hard-pressed neighbors. That same year they bought oil from farmers and ranchers who felt blessed to have a buyer who enabled them to save their farms and ranches. The farmers and ranchers gladly accepted small down-payments with the balance being paid in installments over many years. This added a small but welcome element of leverage to the Perot's investing formula.

In late 2013—after the price of oil had recovered—Ross, Jr. says, "We sold our U.S. oil inventory." Profits were huge. Subsequently, oil prices plummeted.

The earlier reference to developing land shows another component of the Perot vision. Ross Jr. began buying land at the North end of Dallas, an area that was rundown and uninviting. As values declined during the down real estate cycle, Ross Jr. doubled down and bought more. To anchor the development, he bought the Dallas Mavericks to bring activity and people to the American Airlines Center near his Dallas property developments.

Ross Jr.'s vision was focused on the big picture—the development of all his land. Buying the Mavericks team was a strategic ploy in pursuit of his vision.

Clearly there were advantages to owning an NBA team. Ross Jr. talked about what he learned from the likes of Commissioner David Stern, the amazing brand builder, and from Stan Kasten, the smartest, most experienced CEO in professional sports.

Interestingly, he acknowledged that his children enjoyed rubbing elbows with the players and the famous who attended games and parties. But he felt his kids were burdened by having to face friends the day after the loss of a crucial game, perhaps reminiscent of the day after Fortune ran Ross Sr.'s picture on the cover. As soon as the team served its anchoring purpose, Ross Jr. sold control to Mark Cuban. [Perot #19]

Hillwood: Build and Own It—They Will Come

Meanwhile he worked with the city and arranged for development of an airport on his Hillwood properties which was to serve as his matchless gate of entry for imported goods.

He cleverly tied the airport to Perot real properties, providing much-needed space for warehousing, and logistics.

The synergy between the Perot real estate, the Perot business relationships and the new airport was extraordinary. It is now the largest landlocked port of entry in this hemisphere.

This was not "build it and they will come," done without regard for customers' needs combined with passive marketing. Instead, Ross Jr. built to fulfill customers' needs so well as to be compelling. And he did that before the customers recognized the need. That's vision.

In recent years, Ross Jr. has developed ties that enabled him to develop a venture capital arm for the family enterprise.

Venture capitalists employ a variety of criteria to determine which entrepreneurs they will back. Some admit to an element of guessing. Ross Jr. relies in part on intuition in choosing which entrepreneurs to back.

He is also eager to help start-ups in which he invests. For example, Ross told the entrepreneur founder of a firm he has invested in how to make the companies at Hillwood prospects for the start-up's product. What a leg-up for a new company!

This was a brilliant way for Perot to distinguish his venture capital enterprise from that of other venture capitalists. It could only come from the mind of a visionary who grasped the bigger picture with his peripheral vision, and a strong desire to help. [Perot #20]

THE VISION THING

The Perot Vision Is Gaited to Seek Bonanza Profits

Today, Ross Jr. remains risk-willing, but he measures and limits the amount put at risk. He's learned not to hold out for a "dream price" such as $20,000 for a horse that died unsold.

Intuition is more valuable when not a mere guess: when based on experience and when aimed at a sphere where ones knowledge and talents can influence a favorable outcome.

Today, Ross Jr. is willing to take lesser profit off the table, enabling him to make more investments in a variety of new opportunities: Changes in strategies and tactics for sure, but resulting in a more mature outlook learned from his dad.

Ross Jr. used to say that he wished EDS hadn't been sold: "EDS was like the sixth child in our family. I thought I'd always work for EDS." But even though GM dividends never matched the cash flow from EDS, his father was content with having sold EDS and being able to do it all over again in Perot Systems.

Today, Ross Jr. agrees with his father: Accumulated profit reinvested in stock of established companies rarely grows as dramatically as wise investments in less established or in new ventures where the added value of know-how and network improves the odds of success.

Start-Up Fever Beats a Ho-Hum Daily Grind

Another important lesson Ross Jr. learned was that his future wasn't tied to, and his passion wasn't really ignited by a particular business, such as EDS, but the involvement in business itself, more particularly in entrepreneurship.

This was a form of Forest & Trees Vision. He loved being part of the founding of new businesses.

He recalled fondly sitting in the living room watching his Dad working with the early team at EDS and later in the kitchen while his father and the early Perot Systems team planned Perot's second computer business. Even as a kid, he felt the vibes of a start-up's creativity. Like his father, he wasn't terribly interested in running a business's day-by-day operations. Both stayed involved but at a leadership level, with the most capable people they could attract handling the operational routine.

For many sons who succeed to leadership of their families' businesses, it is the existing business that is their adrenaline source. For some it is and should be. However, Ross Jr.'s type of introspection is well advised regardless of the outcome.

Forest & Trees Vision continues to work for Ross Jr. today, albeit now aimed at both the businesses and the individuals.

Much of the Perot success comes from what the two men bring to the table over and above money—contacts, leads, know-how, talent: Intuition in areas where they lack the ability to provide added value likely wouldn't lead to success such as they've achieved. All of this has become part of their shared visions, which drives their business approach.

Vision Chart

(For Chapter 6)

Find inspiration in a prior visionary. If that visionary can't be your parent, find a suitable role model. Then try to meet that person or at least learn all you can about how your adopted visionary achieved success.

Separate your vision from your immediate goals. For Ross Perot Jr., the vision was an efficient way to handle growing imports from Latin America. The property acquisition, the airport and surrounding properties were assets that served the implementation of the vision.

The Vision Transition

Ross Perot, Sr. credits *his* father with teaching him leadership. Ross Perot Jr. credits *his* father with teaching him to be a visionary. Interestingly, Bob Walter's father had arranged a summer vacation job for Bob at Cardinal Foods and later referred Bob to Cardinal when it was for sale. Yet, Bob said he didn't go into the food distribution business because of but despite his father. Where Ross Jr. worships his father, as one might revere the Pope, Walter couldn't acknowledge that he—a Cardinal acolyte—was following his father's suggestions.

CHAPTER 7

Bob Walter

Bob Walter Bet the Food Farm
on a Pharma Harvest

▼▼▼▼▼▼▼▼▼▼▼▼

*O*n an initial base of a borrowed million dollars, Bob Walter used his vision to exploit pricing anomalies in the wholesale grocery trade, then sold out and bet the farm on a hum drum pharma business where he exploited lots of other overlooked wellsprings. Through his series of Beyond-the-Eaves Visionary moves, Bob Walter created signally successful Cardinal Health, a public company now valued at $26 billion.

Bob Walter grew up in a middle class Ohio family. His father, Robert Cecil Walter, was a long-term employee in the food industry. Although Bob was smart, a good college education was possible only because Ohio University offered him a scholarship. He studied engineering, worked hard—harder than anyone else he says—and graduated at the top of his class. [Walter #1] Upon graduating, he married his grade school sweetheart, and to fulfill his financial obligations, took a job in engineering at North American Rockwell. Why? Because, as Bob puts it, "It paid well."

Even before taking the job, he knew he'd hate it. He had determined that big companies lived by rules of seniority and tenure. And Rockwell operated on cost-plus contracts.

Philosophically Bob believed that seniority rules and cost-plus contracts would prevent his advancement on merit.

Tenure contradicted his "work-harder-than-everyone-else-to-get-ahead" ethic. And he couldn't prove his worth by improving efficiencies. In a cost plus environment the employer gets reimbursed regardless of inefficiencies.

Somehow he had concluded that he needed an MBA. Bob was friendly with the president of Ohio University, a result of Bob's academic performance at the school.

The college president encouraged Bob to go to Harvard Business School. By the way, it tells something about Bob that his relationship with his Ohio University president continues. They had lunch days before my interview with Bob for this book. [Walter #2]

Bob wound up in the upper 10 percent of his HBS class. [Walter #3] On the other hand, Bob felt he had only learned how to manage big businesses. HBS offered no courses about running small businesses. Yet, deep down, Bob really wanted to own a small business, somehow, some day. We shall see if this panned out.

Bob returned to Columbus, Ohio where he hoped to buy a business. He felt his local network would make this easier to accomplish. His father was still active in the food industry and his connections were helpful. His dad told him Cardinal Food, a distribution company, was being spun off by what is now the Sara Lee Corporation.

Actually, Bob had worked one summer in the Cardinal warehouse, a job he also got through his father's food industry networking. Interestingly, despite his father having alerted Bob to the availability of Cardinal Food, Bob says he didn't enter the food business because his father was in that industry but in spite of that. He was clearly a man determined to follow his own star.

The acquisition price was only $1,500,000, which was about $1,500,000 more than Bob was worth. He went to several banks, and one of them finally offered to loan $900,000, collateralized by the company's inventory and receivables.

But Bob had no idea where to get $600,000 in equity. Decidedly resourceful, Bob retreated to the Columbus Public Library where he read about Small Business Investment Companies. He found an SBIC in Chicago, LaSalle Capital Group, that was seeking investments such as he needed.

His presentation to LaSalle was well received. The SBIC was willing to invest $435,000. Bob was short $165,000, but no prisoner of false pride, this Harvard MBA went door-to-door to raise the remaining $165,000. [Walter #4]

▼▼▼▼▼▼▼▼▼▼▼▼▼▼▼▼▼▼▼▼▼▼▼▼▼▼▼▼

When Neighbors Became a Crowd

Had Bob Walter made up his financing shortfall in the social media age of today, he might have turned to Crowdfunding rather than going door to door to raise his final $165,000. crowdfunding, much like e-dating services, "introduces" those seeking funds to their lists of investors who invest mostly small amounts in startups and small firms.

▲▲▲▲▲▲▲▲▲▲▲▲▲▲▲▲▲▲▲▲▲▲▲▲▲▲▲▲

This chain of events reflects the early development of Bob's visionary mind. He believed in the value of research, doing his homework and "working harder than anyone else."

Amazingly, no one asked Bob about his exit strategy. More interestingly, he explained that he didn't have one. He simply worked hard to grow his business so as to "make it more saleable." [Walter #5] Fitting his life pattern, he was sure that he could work harder than anyone else and that this would lead to success.

His HBS classmates derided his choice, due to its lack of prestige. They were working for Goldman Sachs, McKinsey and other luminous names in the consulting and investment banking fields. They saw this as a sure-thing route to financial success. To them, it seemed a puzzle that anyone who'd graduated in the top 10 percent of his Harvard Business School class would risk buying a small company that distributed to independent grocers. To his classmates this suggested limited success potential.

Bob's approach was counter-intuitive. He felt that he had minimized risk in search of larger aims: "For me, it wasn't much risk. I had nothing, so I didn't really risk anything other than my career. I thought, 'What the hell,

I might as well do it now. It's going to be harder to do this in five years. I can always get a job.' I was just risking time."

His first years in the business provided the education he didn't get at HBS. As it turned out, Bob was motivated by necessity: the kind that leads the visionary to develop.

So he became innovative. Just twenty-three days after the acquisition closed, the company's union contract expired. [Walter #6]

Bob's instincts kicked in. He managed to negotiate a favorable union contract renewal. He used a sound negotiating trick he developed on his own, namely: "If I'm negotiating and you give me ten arguments against my position, I'm going to find your weakest argument and just blast it away."

Warehouse manager was a key management post for assuring smooth operations. Garnering new customers took time and effort. One warehouse flub could negate such efforts. His warehouse man was "a nice guy," says Bob, but wasn't very communicative in the afternoons. Bob noticed problems in the warehouse that the manager should have prevented. Bob admits that it took longer than it should have for him to realize the guy was an alcoholic. Bob just hadn't experienced anything like that. Once he figured it out, he resolved it deftly. [Walter #7]

Bob's quest to get new customers was at first lacking in strategy. He even syndicated partnership interests in shopping centers he established with anchor tenant grocery stores, thereby literally creating new customers. That approach had serious limitations. Mostly he found ways to help his customers grow, which improved Cardinal's growth. Bob said "it wasn't rapid growth. It was just plugging along, each year doing a bit better." Clearly that was not enough for him.

He wanted to grow the business. But banks were not willing to provide the funds he thought were necessary.

Still he innovated. To improve cash flow, the company started using a bank located in Waco, Texas and one in Anchorage, Alaska. Why? The local Federal Reserve Banks were the slowest at transferring funds. The Fed delays afforded Bob maximum float on disbursements. [Walter #8]

It's no surprise that Bob didn't learn this technique at HBS. Nor is it any surprise that Bob was so innovative.

What is remarkable is the way he analyzed the need, looked elsewhere for solutions and used weaknesses in the system as tools to fix his problems. He was a Beyond-the-Eaves Visionary. Bob has made his visionary approach a business staple —studying other businesses and figuring how to use their wisdom or failings to improve his situation.

Initially Bob believed that good homework and hard work were all he needed. While he still believed that mantra, his outlook was changing. He understood that ideas from other bright people could be more valuable than his own. He exploited this mind set by seeking out ways of doing things that worked in other industries. So he used a Forest & Trees Vision to see where and how he could profit from new opportunities while keeping his eyes on operations. He used a Beyond-the-Eaves Vision to understand and replicate others' best ideas, while still minding his own business issues.

Many business leaders look at others to determine "best practices" that they can then copy and replicate. Bob did not want to be like others but to better them, in effect: better than best.

Along the way, Bob studied the supermarket business, his direct customers. He noticed that "half the products were on sale each week, and the supermarkets' customers seemed to buy only what was on sale." Further he figured that "for this to happen, the manufacturers had to be giving promotional allowances on merchandise with extended shelf life. Those discounts approximated 20 percent."

Bob viewed those discounts as a cost reduction. He knew he could take advantage of this system but had to find a way to avoid the downside of carrying too much inventory too long. To maximize the profitability on such circumstances, he had to be able to predict how much and when stores would buy in periods between promotions.

Then he could stock up on the promoted goods and either improve his margin of profit or beat competitors' prices during those interim months when those items were fully-priced on his competitors' shelves. For this, he employed Trend Pattern Vision.

Clearly, Bob had spotted an opportunity—a result of his homework, and of Beyond-the-Eaves and Trend Pattern Visions. (Keep in mind that if the predictions were wrong, he would take a bath.) [Walter #9]

He was halfway there. However, merely having a good idea isn't enough. And dropping a great idea because of the potential downside is only half way to an innovation. Most would do just that—drop a great idea, explaining their action with an analogy like, "If pigs had wings, they could fly." Bob had no need for a lame withdrawal excuse. Bob wasn't satisfied going halfway with an innovation. He needed to solve the problem of precisely predicting retailers' purchasing habits.

To do that, he searched for and hired a fellow, Doug Linton, who had no experience in the food industry. But Linton had a master's degree from Carnegie Mellon in operations research. Bob explained the situation and instructed Doug to develop algorithms to exploit it.

But he didn't make Linton a researcher. Oh no. He made him head of purchasing. That was totally unorthodox. But this was a great way to imprint Bob's visionary mind on the key members of his team. He told Doug that he viewed the discounted inventory as an investment on which he wanted to make money by properly timing the buying and selling. [Walter #10]

Sounds simple. But it was truly brilliant—so much so that no one else figured it out. Even Bob's classmates' firms, such as the venerable McKinsey & Co., didn't spot this opportunity.

McKinsey provided consulting to the food industry's top players. Indeed, no one figured it out for years. Meanwhile, Bob used the system to great advantage.

It's important to note that although Bob had the vision and even the strategy, he acknowledges that he couldn't have pulled it off alone. He gives credit to Doug Linton and to others on his team. That's fair, but they couldn't have helped if Bob hadn't imbued them with his vision.

Growth Is Key to Landing and Retaining Top Hires

Most people would use the Linton hiring as an example of the widely quoted thesis, "If you get good people, they will enable you to grow." Bob says, "That's backwards. You must grow in order to get good people. Because if I'm going to come to your company and you're not a growth company, I have to step on the next guy to get a job promotion which for most of us is distasteful. So, you've got to grow doing new things, and keep on growing to keep the good people." [Walter #11]

Matters progressed. Bob got Cardinal to grow each year, enough so that he paid off his bank debt and bought out many investors. He wound up with nearly 70% of the company, but the business's growth was incremental. He constantly landed customers formerly served by bigger distributors. Despite working at least as hard as anyone in the industry, Bob felt growth was slow.

For most players, Bob's success would have been worthy of celebration. In a relatively short time, he'd gone from zero net worth to a net worth equal to more than 70 percent of Cardinal's increased value. And Cardinal was now debt-free. But it wasn't fast enough nor big enough for Bob.

He was stymied in his efforts to create exponential growth in his industry. Not his fault: the food distribution business had consolidated to a point at which lucrative opportunities were unavailing. He certainly looked for such opportunities. But properties he could afford were not worth buying.

It was obvious to Bob that Cardinal's distribution skills were applicable to other industries. So he considered becoming a distributor in another

industry. He explored hardware. He saw little promise there. Looking elsewhere, he convinced Coors Beer to give him a limited geographic franchise. [Walter #12]

▼▼▼▼▼▼▼▼▼▼▼▼▼▼▼▼▼▼▼▼▼▼▼▼▼▼▼▼▼▼▼▼▼▼▼▼▼

It's the Big Idea That Counts: Don't Get Waylaid

Fortunately, Bob didn't stop there. He didn't consider Coors his silver bul-
let (the theme of the famous Coors TV ad). This is worthy of deeper analysis. Having an innovative idea and making it work, such as getting the
Coors franchise, often makes people focus on that one idea, ignoring other
ideas. Bob's horizons were wider than that. So he kept studying; kept thinking. He needed a big idea and a change in direction. His radar scanned
other industries and companies, all the while focused on running his current business—a great example of Beyond-the-Eaves and Forest and Eaves
Visions.

▲▲▲▲▲▲▲▲▲▲▲▲▲▲▲▲▲▲▲▲▲▲▲▲▲▲▲▲▲▲▲▲▲▲▲▲

Eventually, he settled on pharmaceuticals distribution. In those days,
drug stores were mostly independent. He had done well with independent grocers, and there were parallels although they weren't obvious to the
casual observer or for that matter, even to industry experts.

At that time, 1980, there were two large distributors and 435 separate
pharma distributors. And since they had to be licensed, it was pretty easy
for Bob to find them. He couldn't buy them all. How was he to figure which
ones to target? [Walter #13]

He reasoned that northeast geography could work to his advantage.
He noted that an area in the northeast U.S. was somewhat protected,
being bounded on the north by Canada (from which drugs could not be

imported) and by mountains on the west and south, which made trucking into the heavily populated area difficult and expensive. [Walter #14]

He started by buying one of the distributors in that region. But with limited capital, he had to find a leg-up advantage. Remember, his reason for moving into the pharma industry was that distribution—the skill he'd developed in food—was readily applicable to the pharma industry. So he revved up what I call Forest & Trees Vision and Beyond-the-Eaves Vision to examine the industries' purchasing systems, even as he learned his new business.

There weren't discount patterns such as those in food. There was, however, an interesting phenomenon. Beyond-the-Eaves Vision kicked into gear. In those days, there were few generic drugs. Given the proliferation of new medicines and their patent protection, together with physicians' tendency to prescribe by name, no wonder the inflation rate in medicine grew at more than twice the rate of the economy as a whole. Bob believed this anomaly could be converted into the equivalent of the food manufacturer discounts.

Bob asked Doug Linton to develop algorithms for the drug industry that would yield data that revealed to Cardinal what, when and how much retailers would buy. Once again, that would tell Bob how much to buy. If you could be reasonably sure that the product price would increase by 20 percent during a given period of time, then buying immediately provided a 20 percent discount at the time of actual sale.

Once again, Bob had determined a way to reduce the cost of his purchases. Even if Cardinal's demand calculations were wrong, there was downside protection.

He could wait until the medicine was out-of-date. Pharmaceutical companies allowed a full refund on out of date drugs. (Note: that loss ceiling didn't compensate for the cost of long-term inventory carry; it merely prevented disasters.) Bob "locked in" an effective cost discount, which no one else figured out. Bob's vision made it available, and he was brave enough to tackle it, too. [Walter #15]

His goal was simply to acquire companies in his target geographic area and convert their existing sales into higher margin sales. If Bob saw a company with $1 million income, acquiring it would likely cost $6 million, the six times income formula being standard back then. However, if he could increase the income to $2.5 million, using his algorithmically determined effective discount, that would mean Bob's acquisition cost was 2.4 times income, rather than 6 times income. Bob couldn't afford not to buy such companies.

However, he didn't have the money to do so. Worse yet, his competition for those acquisition targets were the six largest distributors. They were all public companies. They could buy companies in exchange for their publicly traded stock. For that they only needed a printing press that created "cheap currency" for buyouts. If Cardinal was to play with the big boys, he needed comparable currency. It was time for Bob to take his growing company public.

So he went public, giving Cardinal a $27 million market cap. The IPO proceeds did enable some internal growth. But more importantly it provided a different kind of (cheap) currency: stock in a public company.

For acquisitions, this was an invaluable asset for a company that had a profit strategy as good as Bob's.

This enabled Cardinal to acquire companies but not as cheaply as Bob wished. Cardinal's stock price was too low for that. Cardinal's stock price was, like his acquisition targets, also determined by the company's income, but over 80 percent of Cardinal's income was food-based.

The market valued drugs more than it did food. Cardinal's stock price was effectively devalued by the lower multiple applied to valuing food businesses. Bob's activities were guided by his vision which was focused on longer term goals.

He continued to build the drug side, acquiring more pharma companies. It was clearly time to focus totally on the pharmaceutical side of the business.

▼▼▼▼▼▼▼▼▼▼▼▼▼▼▼▼▼▼▼▼▼▼▼▼▼▼▼▼▼▼▼▼

Skills and Appetite Exceeded Food Industry Potential

Bob had spent nearly a decade building a food distribution business. That business not only supported his family, it largely repaid his backers, increasing Bob's net worth accordingly. Everyone would have defined Bob as a food industry guy; yet he saw himself as a distribution guy, which opened broader vistas for his vision. Forest & Trees Vision enabled him to distribute drugs, as well as food. So when the opportunity arose, when Beyond-the-Eaves and Trend Pattern Visions led him to believe the drug industry had greater potential, Bob pounced. As this suggests, he was clearly a multi-faceted visionary.

The pharma vision whetted his appetite; food was no longer sufficient, so he promptly disposed of the earthbound food business. The drug industry was consolidating rapidly, and he was eager to exploit that opportunity while it still existed.

The key: Know what you are. You may be defined by your industry but may have strengths and skills that transcend your industry. That's part of Forest & Trees Vision. It takes good homework and self-appraisal to determine that. It may require external help, but ultimately only you can digest the input and make the decision.

▲▲▲▲▲▲▲▲▲▲▲▲▲▲▲▲▲▲▲▲▲▲▲▲▲▲▲▲▲▲▲▲

Bob wasn't through. By virtue of intellectual curiosity and drive, he discovered yet another flaw in the system.

That flaw enabled pharma manufacturers to bypass distributors. The manufacturers were selling bulk medicine directly to the chains. The chains then encompassed only 40 percent of the market. (It is more like 90 percent now.)

The manufacturer would sell the chains bags of 5,000 pills of certain medicines at a significantly lower price. The chains would then repackage putting 100 pills into bottles and send the bottles to their stores.

The manufacturers used the excuse that they saved the cost of putting the meds into more bottles. But the effect was to grant a discount to the retailers, a margin far greater than the chains' actual handling costs. That margin normally would have belonged to distributors like Cardinal.

Bob wanted the same deal. So he approached the manufacturers. But he was told they couldn't sell 5,000 pill bags to him because Cardinal wasn't a retailer. This wasn't just about volume: it also affected the retailers' margins.

Told of the barriers—that he was not a retailer and that he lacked the necessary experts to become one—Bob hired experienced retail people and qualified for the pill bagging program. The manufacturers had no choice. They sold their 5000 pill bags to Cardinal. Bob put Doug Linton, the algorithm man, in charge and started selling rebottled meds to independent retail drug stores.

Soon Cardinal was doing it so efficiently and with such scale that Bob's company was selling rebottled meds to CVS and Walgreen's. Eventually, the manufacturers realized they no longer benefited by helping the chains and they were giving away margin. Program terminated: But not before Cardinal had experienced a highly-profitable ten year run. [Walter #16]

By this time, Cardinal Health had saturated its targeted geographic region. Beyond-the-Eaves Vision told Bob his best route for serious expansion would be to enter the closely related hospital market.

But again Cardinal lacked necessary expertise. Where to find it? He targeted James W. Daly Inc., a company in Boston that had the needed skills. In fact, Daly had what Bob described as "an incredible reputation in the hospital market. The purchase price was $32 million—cash.

That's because Daly would not take Cardinal stock. Were Bob to pay cash, his company would be at-risk, seriously at-risk. Cardinal's market cap—the aggregate value of all its shares at then current per share market price—was $30 million. The buy would leave Bob completely leveraged.

And Bob knew James W. Daly had made a serious error. It expanded its union contracts to cover all operations. Yet he did the deal. (It took ten years to fix the union problem.)

Betting the Farm and Changing Approach Mid-Bet

Remember, Bob had no net worth when he acquired Cardinal Foods. He rationalized that it would be harder some time in the future to take such a risk when he had a lot to lose. Well, "some time in the future" had arrived.

He bet the farm to acquire the expertise to grow his company through the hospital market. Of course, no one had a gun to his head saying, "Grow or die." Yet the way Bob felt, there might as well have been such a gun.

Bob knew that his ability to attract and retain top talent was dependent on growth—exponential growth. Growth was not a choice: it was a necessity. His choice was whether to grow by new geography, which meant directly challenging larger, entrenched competitors, or by entering new niche markets. The decision was easy: new markets.

Remember, Bob spent heavily taking Cardinal public to gain cheap currency for acquisitions. He'd made that strategy publicly known. Many would feel compelled to prove the validity of their strategy. Rapid Action Vision dictated a "no alternative" but to buy Daly, no matter how risky a cash deal seemed. Crazy? No. Bob was too smart to forsake an opportunity that was consistent with his vision regarding growth just to feed his ego regarding a clever strategy. So he kept the cheap currency in his pocket and used precious cash to buy Daly.

The decision turned out to be brilliant. The year before the acquisition, Daly's revenue was $135 million. During the following year, Cardinal's then new hospital division landed two new customers: a large hospital group and the New England VHA, which increased revenue by 60-70 percent. This could not have occurred without the expertise and reputation of James W. Daly Inc. That and the "locked-in" effective Cardinal's discount methods made the company's move into the hospital niche a home run deal. This also made Cardinal Health a new power in the field.

Once Cardinal was in the hospital market, Bob found an extraordinary cure to a more or less standard inefficiency. Nurses had always ordered meds for their patients from the hospital pharmacy. The pharmacist prepared the meds and sent them to the nursing station. It was inefficient. In an adroit move, based on Forest & Trees and Beyond-the-Eaves Visions, Cardinal acquired Pyxis, a fast-growing tech concern that enabled Cardinal to set up medicine "ATMs" at hospital nursing stations. The automated med stations were a huge success.

Make the Sum of the Parts Greater Than the Whole

The hospital industry is huge. Most hospitals had been small businesses. Most purveyors to hospitals viewed them as distinct small businesses. Bob recognized that small hospitals' pharmacies weren't competing with those of nearby hospitals. So each was willing to let him deal with the others, and that enabled him to wrest the advantages as though dealing with one monster hospital while actually dealing with all the small ones. That prompted him to find and buy Pyxis, whose new technology enabled Cardinal to capture and retain a huge market share. That's another example from Bob of the bottom line value of using Beyond-the-Eaves Vision to know a customer's business even better than the customer does.

▼▼▼▼▼▼▼▼▼▼▼▼▼▼▼▼▼▼▼▼▼▼▼▼▼▼▼▼▼▼▼▼

Discovering an Idea Is Not Enough: So Then What?

When I asked Bob the secret to his success, he explained that he never originated an idea. "All I did was figure out who is really smart, determine what they're doing and tweak their idea to make it just a little better."

That may be an accurate overview but is hardly complete. It was clear to me that Bob and his team did a couple of additional things: They did great homework, finding exceptional sources of information and carefully studying what they gleaned from those sources. In their quest to understand what was going on in their industry, they gained valuable insights. These were insights that had not occurred to others. Bob did something, almost by instinct, that I've been teaching my Kellogg students and consulting clients to do for decades: future success belongs to those who incorporate multiple disciplines into their business strategies. Doing so elevates creativity. [Walter #17]

This skill—bringing together variegated areas and viewing a unique combined perspective—is similar to that used by Kay Koplovitz.

For example, experientially enhancing distribution capabilities in itself helped Cardinal's operating success. Similarly, spotting the potential of industry discounts in the food industry and the effect of price inflation in the pharmaceutical industry presented unique opportunities.

But the opportunities were just that and nothing more without the new discipline: algorithmic predictability. Once he added that, he gained sufficient advantage to allow a bet-the-farm strategy. Keep in mind that he didn't have to bet the farm to do well. He chose the higher level of risk because success could bring fabulous rewards that were not attainable had he relied on the traditional approach, because his algorithmic approach managed the risk better than his competitors could do. That effectively reduced his comparative risks. Because Bob was ever the food and drug distributor, he recognized that innovative ideas also have limited shelf lives.

You may be more risk averse than Bob Walter. But you can emulate his visionary genius. Bob said Harvard Business School did not teach him anything about running a small business. It's clear, though, that he learned key lessons through an innovative approach that took advantage of the shortcomings of normal business practice. He saw others shackled by conventional business practices and limitations, as well as how those limitations could help him pursue his vision. He creatively employed technology to negate the otherwise inherent clash between his and others' visions. His sense of the world gave him confidence that his prior study and hard work would pay off. By employing those practices, Cardinal's value snowballed. He made his small business an industry giant in the process.

THE VISION THING

Cardinal's Bob Walter: A Visionary's Visionary

Was Bob a better visionary than the others I interviewed? No, it's not a matter of better. It is about Bob's ability to own so many elements of vision. His vision elements run the gamut of four of the five I have identified: Beyond-the-Eaves, Forest & Trees, Trend Pattern and Rapid Action Visions.

In addition and quite remarkably he was a *serial* visionary. The odds are against being able to see one vision after another and then apply a bet-the-farm approach. Yet, that seems reasonable when you realize, as Bob did, that others weren't seeing what he saw.

Bob also was endowed with the ability to combine various disciplines. This is not unlike Kay Koplovitz. Those Baby Boomers who exhibited such skills were unique and had a leg-up on others of that generation. As I've told my students and clients for decades, being able to combine two disciplines, either by dint of one's own knowledge or by joining with other(s), will become the minimum essential behavior of successful millennial business visionaries. It will be a prerequisite for big success. Be warned!

Vision Chart

(For Chapter 7)

▶ Know your business well, but be curious about other businesses and their successes.

▶ Do smart homework until you know more than anyone else knows about the topic. It helps if you can address a market where this is feasible.

▶ If you don't know how to achieve your vision, figure out what skills you need, where to find them, and how to attract them in terms of people who possess them.

The Vision Transition

Bob Walter was a great example of a business visionary who used extraordinary means to make his vision feasible. It is difficult to know whether others weren't willing to try such aggressive and new techniques, such as algorithms. It is entirely possible that they simply never saw the possibilities, which of course is an example of challenged vision.

Like Walter, Eitan Wertheimer also felt comfortable going where no non-U.S. business had gone before: in his case, to the Oracle of Omaha.

Unlike Bob who chose his first industry despite his father's presence in that industry, Eitan was loyal to his father's vision that Iscar should be a capitalistic business with a semi-socialistic bent, at least regarding employees.

CHAPTER 8

Eitan Wertheimer

Some Visionaries Need
an Oracle Assist

▼▼▼▼▼▼▼▼▼▼▼

*I*t was a plan that seemed futile on its face. How could the leader of Iscar, a high tech Israeli metal tooling firm get an investment titan across the sea in America to buy a family-owned firm tethered to a kibbutz mentality by his father's covenant to save the workers' jobs? The bigger question is why his son Eitan would focus on Warren Buffett, who had built his enormous wealth buying only American firms? Buffett shunned what he did not understand. Eitan Wertheimer didn't know Omaha, Nebraska, Buffett's U.S. base from, say, Hebron, Ohio. There were so many potential buyers, some of whom might pay more. Why was an oracle more important to a visionary than more money?*

Giving an Oracle a Telescope

When Warren Buffett was in business school at Columbia University, he walked into the office of one of the most influential investment advisors ever, Benjamin Graham. Graham was the author of *The Intelligent Investor*,

127

read by every serious investment management student since the mid-20ᵗʰ century.

Graham's specialty was security analysis—matching the liabilities of individual companies against their assets. When a firm's value per share was significantly below that of net assets, Graham favored the stock. Simple? Yes, but nuanced enough that Graham found myriad values that were overlooked by investors.

Buffett was eager to work for the master. He asked Graham for a job. Graham turned him down: "I'd work for nothing," said Buffett: "You'd be overpaid," Graham said.

Graham eventually hired Buffett who was—and is—so successful the Nebraska native is known as The Oracle of Omaha.

Though he has had losses like everyone else, his record is spectacular. He is a true visionary. His Berkshire Hathaway investments in undervalued companies have made him one of the world's richest billionaires.

Buffett favors companies that are outstanding in their field. One day, Buffett was approached by Eitan Wertheimer who had written to Buffett from abroad to offer the Oracle of Omaha an unorthodox deal by Buffett's standards. Eitan was in fact the CEO of a concern that *was* outstanding in its field. But his company, Iscar, was based in Israel. Buffett had never bought a foreign-based company before. What's more, Buffett would have to accept a dictate: the workers had to retain their jobs.

Until 2006, Buffet's expertise had been tested in only the United States. In much the same way he famously excluded high tech as being outside his area of knowledge, he clearly seemed comfortable investing only in his home country.

When Buffet received Eitan Wertheimer, he had never before met the Israeli who ran Iscar. (This Israel-based business was founded by Eitan's father, Stef.) More meetings followed, and Eitan convinced the Oracle of Omaha to expand his horizon. His letter sent prior to his visit, was a personal one-on-one message. It was, in effect, the catalyst by which one visionary convinced another to buy control of a company founded by still a third visionary. That may sound reminiscent of Churchill's, "It is a riddle, wrapped in a mystery, inside an enigma," but here there is no enigma.

The Capitalist Kibbutz Company

In 1937, eleven year-old Stef Wertheimer fled the Nazis with his family and moved to Israel. By age 16, he had dropped out of school. He had two stints in the military, first for the Brits during World War II and later in Israel's pre-state Haganah (defense) Army. Then he went to work for Rafael, the military armament company owned by the State of Israel. But he was soon dismissed due to his lack of formal schooling.

In 1952, he started a metal tooling business in his back yard. That business later became Iscar. It didn't take long for Stef's business to catch the attention of Discount Investment, the investment arm of Israel's third largest bank. Iscar tools were superb. The company grew to have operations in over 50 countries and captured a significant share of the global market.

Stef was a good businessman, which has many components. One of those had to do with his being an Israeli in pre and post state status. In those days, Israel was largely socialist. Founded by immigrants from the Soviet Union, the kibbutz mentality—the well-known Israeli commune— was engrained in the young country's moral and social fiber.

Stef built Iscar with that cultural background in place. When I interviewed him in the late 1980s, for my first book, *Entrepreneurs Are Made Not Born*, he referred to Iscar as a "capitalist kibbutz company."

Stef believed that he owed each of his employees the security due to fellow builders of his company.

He had a vision, a Beyond-the-Eaves Vision, that, first of all, caused him to treat his employees in much the same way as Israeli citizens were then treated by their government. Beyond-the-Eaves Vision was also grounded in the Wertheimers' view of maternity, where mothers guide their children's development by balancing authority and responsibility. Good mothers also balance close-to-the-skirt management with granting kids greater freedom. As Eitan noted, they learned that "every time we did nothing, we were perfect." [Wertheimer #1]

Furthermore, Forest & Trees Vision told him that by doing so, he would earn the long-term loyalty of his employees. They would appreciate his giving them the opportunity to continually improve their skills and thus would increase Iscar's capability. Besides, it seemed the right thing to do.

Stef's vision, albeit developed and applied within Israeli culture, was indeed unique even in Israel. Except for companies owned by the Histadrut, the country's supreme labor union, no other company of any size was run like Iscar. And the Histadrut did not fare well, proving ill-equipped or excessively saddled by its socialistic business principles. Yet Stef's Iscar thrived.

Stef's vision was excellent and his ability to implement within his vision's constraint was exemplary. However, not even Stef realized how much he and his family would be constrained by his vision, nor ultimately, how they would benefit from it.

Prodigal Son: The Heir that Filled the Sail

Stef's only son, Eitan, also dropped out of high school. Eitan's short stint at Iscar—to fix an ailing plant—was deferred due to compulsory military service when he was deployed to Lebanon in the 1982 war. When he finally returned, he fixed that plant but wanted to leave and build his own business—turning around underperforming companies. That reaction was partially Eitan's nature but was somewhat precipitated by Stef's way of dealing with Eitan. Although Eitan had done a very good job, doubling production at the once ailing plant, the most Stef could give Eitan when he asked his father, "Did I do OK?" was: "Your customers will tell you, and the people you work with will tell you. The facts will talk. So it doesn't matter what I say." [Wertheimer #2]

In late 1982, Eitan left to tour in China. He told me that, a few days into 1983, he received a call that his father had "a very big auto accident, that he had some [unspecified] damage in the head, and that I should come quickly home."

It turned out that Stef had a very severe concussion. Eitan's mother told him he had to run the business. Stef recovered several months later but had to undergo therapy for speech and other accident-related issues.

Stef asked Eitan to continue running the business. The way he asked was odd: "Listen, you did not bad and would you stay and continue running Iscar?" Eitan agreed to do so if he could be totally in charge. He committed to stay for ten years: "If I'm not good, you can kick me out any day you want. I will keep you informed. But I don't want anyone telling me what to do."

Eitan did very well indeed. He took Iscar from 52nd to 2nd in the market. He grew the business far more than he had projected to Stef. As his ten years was ending, Stef had found more projects needing Eitan's attention. One was of prime import:

Iscar, in a joint venture with Pratt & Whitney, expanded into the business of making turbine blades for jet engines. This was after the Six Day War. Israel had needed a reserve supply.

In early 1995, Eitan stepped back into a sort of chairman position, to allow his second in command, Jacob Harpaz, a non-family executive, to assume the leadership role. For six months, Eitan stayed away, to give Jacob some room. Then he started coming in primarily to ask questions. A disagreement with Discount Investments, led Eitan to buy out the bank. This took more of his time. That issue went to the Israel Supreme Court.

As time went on, Eitan realized that Iscar was facing a succession issue. Eitan had five children; his siblings another six. No one in his family's third generation asked to run Iscar.

Iscar had become a large global operation that was very complex to operate. Under ordinary circumstances, someone in Eitan's shoes would have hired a top investment banking firm to find the buyer who would pay the most to acquire Iscar. But these were anything but ordinary circumstances.

In 2006, Iscar was the realization of his father, Stef's vision. The Wertheimers would be the first to confirm that Iscar's success was largely attributable to the dedication and skills of their employees. But that resulted from Stef's management philosophy, advanced by Eitan. It was based on loyalty and commitment to help employees be far better than they otherwise could have been. Willingly, Eitan was an accessory after the fact—saddled with his father's vision.

He couldn't just sell to the highest bidder, because such a buyer might well conclude that new employees would cost less or even that the profits could be enhanced by moving Iscar's headquarters out of Israel. After all, the company had operations in over 50 countries. A sale to a new owner with no emotional ties to Israel and without Stef's socialistic sentiments would end the sense of loyalty and security enjoyed by Iscar employees.

Eitan was balancing on the horns of a dilemma. Family businesses always straddle allegiances to family and to the family business. Such a paradox is quite common. Here, the paradox was in spades: A vision, a founder's vision endorsed by his successor son, colliding with the needs of the owner's family with the bulk of its wealth tied up in the family business.

Eitan's only solution: use Retro Vision to identify and enforce the family's values and a way-Beyond-the-Eaves Vision that was big enough to encompass both: find someone who could buy Iscar and who would honor and maintain Stef's vision for the foreseeable future. Eitan's vision grasped the possible relevance of the Oracle of Omaha, Warren Buffet. [Wertheimer #3]

But Eitan did not know Omaha, let alone the Oracle. He could have retained an intermediary. But he knew the prospect of Buffet buying Iscar, if it were to happen, would not be solely a financial transaction. Buffet had teams to handle the financial and legal aspects of acquisitions. Important steps preceded getting to those aspects. Only Warren Buffet might appreciate the sensitivities and the value of those underlying values.

So Eitan wrote a personal letter to Buffet. He spelled out the special relationship between Iscar and its employees. He explained how important that had been and how it formed the basis upon which his father and later Eitan had built this extraordinarily profitable company. It worked. They met, and before long, the deal was done. [Wertheimer #4] Berkshire Hathaway made its first acquisition outside the U.S. It bought the "capitalist kibbutz company" called Iscar. The Oracle of Omaha was convinced by Eitan, the Retro Visionary to buy a firm set up by his father, a unique visionary in a land of biblical visions.

The Oracle of Omaha was quite accustomed to broad media coverage. The acquisition of an Israeli company garnered coverage by media that Buffet had never before experienced, including the "Jewish Chronicle" in Australia. When he learned of that, Warren told Eitan, tongue in cheek, "I never got such media coverage in my life. Until I met you, I was nobody." [Wertheimer #5]

THE VISION THING
A Snowball Sailing Through the Desert

Stef clearly had visions of Iscar continuing as a family business. He called on son, Eitan to help run the business, even before Stef's accident made that somewhat compelling. His inability to praise Eitan's good results or to offer a long-term commitment likely reflects Stef's reluctance to let go.

Some visions begin small and humble, only later becoming profound. Those visions snowball, although those snowballs' paths generally resemble sailboats' tacking. Today, Israel has some snow, and a surprising number of masts dot its harbors. Still, neither is particularly symbolic of Israel, but they do demonstrate change. Those who ignore change are in peril, whether that change is ahead or behind them.

Stef founded Iscar when Israel was more like a desert. His vision of continuity was not unreasonable, but believing he or even his family could run it forever was wishful thinking, a mirage in the midst of a desert.

Vision Chart

(For Chapter 8)

▶ Changing times may necessitate new, additional visions, but needn't mean abandoning earlier visions. Eitan had new visions about disposing of the business that could honor his and his father's vision.

▶ Thinking out of the box is often a good idea if you're trying to reconcile multiple visions. That may be more challenging, but there are circumstances that make "out-of-the-box" a necessity. Warren Buffett only bought American companies, yet Eitan comfortably left the box's protection and wrote a highly-persuasive personal letter to Buffet.

The Vision Transition

Having a vision, even a great vision, may not be sufficient. It generally must be in the hands of someone who can articulate it and select the right people to help implement it.

Eitan Wertheimer used Retro Vision to reach back to the "kibbutz capitalistic" vision and principles: loyalty to employees, that his father, Stef, whom he loved, used upon founding Iscar. Eitan did so because he believed it would help to honor that vision, while also benefiting his family, current and later generations.

Rick Waddell didn't even realize he loved the Northern Trust. Yet, he used Retro Vision to reach back to the company's values, in order to benefit current customers. Initially, Northern Trust's key people, Waddell included, took a huge hit. The risk was far greater than the apparent benefit.

CHAPTER 9

Rick Waddell

Rick Waddell: CEO Takes Northern Trust on a Fateful Journey

▼▼▼▼▼▼▼▼▼▼▼▼

66 **W**e have financial strength, a great balance sheet, and lots of liquidity. We need to step up and use the financial strength of the bank to support our clients in this very tough time. That's what Northern Trust does. It's the right thing to do."

Caught in the grip of a financial debacle, Rick Waddell did not back away from his responsibilities as he saw them. He paid customers their due even though the bank had not earned the money. He used the bank reserves and forfeited management's anticipated bonuses including his own. Could the embattled CEO survive apparent excesses believed to be scandalous by his many critics?

The CEO's Other Love Did Not Deceive His Wife

Rick Waddell has long admitted to having a long-term, passionate love affair with a lady other than his wife.

In 2009, about eighteen months after becoming CEO of The Northern Trust Company, he proceeded to act out of character for the head of one of America's most conservative banks, risking his job and the reputation of his love object.

No, this chapter does not belong in the National Enquirer. Rick's passionate love affair was with the Grey Lady, which is how people refer to The Northern Trust Company He loved the bank and his job, although in truth not as much as he loved his wife, but he really did risk all by the unusual move he made in 2009.

There was method in his madness: Rick had extraordinary Retro Vision, which enabled him to capture the values, culture and raison d'etre for Northern Trust's very existence. It was not obvious to critics of bankers' ways and seemed contrary even to the policies of the federal government. However, Rick's vision was unwavering, and he acted to pursue it and to be resolutely faithful to that vision.

Before explaining what Rick did, it's important first to reflect on the dramatic economic circumstances of the years 2008-2009 and on the Grey Lady's special banking attributes.

Those years kicked off the worst recession since the Great Depression of the 1930s. The Great Recession arose out of a period during which many banks were irresponsible in their lending practices. Millions of individuals had been granted mortgages they could not afford: foreclosures abounded. A ripple effect put the nation's finances in such jeopardy that rescue seemed unattainable.

However, Northern Trust is unlike most banks. It doesn't make much money the way most banks do: by lending money. The bulk of Northern Trust's profits derive from providing asset management and advisory services to wealthy individuals and organizations. Its Federal capital requirements aren't measurable in the same way as are those of traditional banks. Other banks' risk assumptions depend on the actual value of their loans.

Risk is based on the likelihood of customers repaying the loans the banks have made.

In the troubled years 2008-9, the U.S. Government had to deal with the bad loan policies that had been adopted by the nation's traditional banks. Regulators feared vast numbers of bad loans in the system might bring down banks, both big and small.

If so, this could torpedo the world's commerce and finance. The government's solution was to loan money to the banks. Of course, it was important that all the banks borrow, lest the stronger ones that didn't borrow would thus be identified as stronger and gain undue advantage. It was a Federal lending policy driven by needs of the weak banks. That was the deal: All banks, weak and strong, *had* to borrow.

Northern Trust faced a dilemma. Northern Trust did not need the loan and explained why to U. S. regulators. Yet the government insisted that it borrow the funds. The Grey Lady was given no choice. So borrow she did.

The following year, 2009, Northern Trust continued to sponsor the PGA golf tournament in Los Angeles, California, pursuant to its five year contract to do so. Attendant to the tournament and consistent with prior practice, there were glamorous parties and festivities. But all hell broke loose thereafter. Northern Trust was accused of "using government money to entertain," while the country suffered the effects of the ongoing Great Recession.

The facts were ignored. Northern Trust was merely doing what it was contractually bound to do. And consider the upside for the system: The PGA generated $35 million in *much needed* economic stimulus. The money was paid out of Northern Trust's income; its 'borrowed money' had never left Fed coffers.

But the fallout was demeaning for the man who had spent over three decades with the bank he now served as CEO. How bad was the fallout? Widely-read TMZ.com carried a headline reading: "Bailout Bank Blows Millions Partying in L.A."

"I received a very nasty letter from 15 Congressmen," Waddell told me, "They demanded that we pay the money back. I wrote them back and said: 'Well, if you read the rules, we're not allowed to pay you back because the Administration hasn't opined on how to pay it back.'

"The Fed was still writing the rules. So I'm sitting there saying, 'What is this big hubbub about? We're doing the right things.'"

Besides, for Rick Waddell, protecting the Grey Lady with whom he'd had a 33-year affair was more than just being a gentleman. It was a matter of being true to a vision which he had adopted, a vision which grew to be his own. Thus, when people made heated, hateful remarks—"the PR was ugly"—Rick was "angry and confused." Sure, that was personally hurtful to Rick Waddell, but more so, it was an affront to his love object. [Waddell #1]

"We paid them back on June 17, 2009, at a 14.5% return to the U.S. tax-payer. Pretty darn good return. I would say 99.9% of Northern Trust clients were right behind us. But we received so many ugly letters, voicemails… from the public…who didn't know Northern Trust from anybody."

When I asked Rick how that mattered to him, given that he knew he and the bank had done the right thing, he said: "because I'm the CEO of one of the good guys." Spoken from the heart, like one defending the reputation of his true love. [Waddell #2]

That wasn't the only way Northern Trust was affected by the Great Recession. Remember that one of the bank's primary functions was managing customers' funds. In 2008, Northern Trust managed over $110 billion in short-term assets as custodian for myriad customers.

Because of the extreme volatility at that time, it was impossible to get meaningful pricing of such assets. When they did get pricing, it generally turned out to be wrong by the time customers wanted to sell. In addition, some clients had purchased auction-rate securities, that were re-priced by a dozen investment banking firms on a daily basis.

These were, Rick said "Very much like a money market fund— with daily liquidity—but the underlying assets were all 5, 7, 10 year pieces of paper, all highly rated. But in 2008, the remarketing dried up. All the investment banks pulled back and said, 'We're not going to put this on our balance sheet.' And the liquidity dried up. We didn't originate or sell those securities. But many of our clients had them because they got a little higher yield.

"We had a lot of clients calling us, saying: 'I can't get my money out of my account, and I have bills to pay.' We concluded: 'Look, we have financial strength, a great balance sheet, and lots of liquidity. We need to step up and use the financial strength of the bank to support our clients in this very tough time. That's what Northern Trust does. It's the right thing to do.'"

That sounds straightforward and sensible, "step up and... support our clients"—what could possibly be wrong with that?

The fact is that 2009 was not a time for sensible, logical thinking in the financial industry. Virtually all the banks in the world were being bombarded one way or another.

No banker felt he could afford to take any chances. After all, some of the biggest commercial and investment banks had failed or were on life-support. Banking was never a place for bravery or aggressive positions. Much like the saying about airplane pilots: there are risk-taking bankers and bankers who survive, but there are few risk-taking bankers who survive.

In 2009, almost all bankers were hunkering down. They certainly weren't standing up for what they considered to be the right thing. After all, they understood that it's the spouting whale that gets harpooned.

In his day-to-day banking functions before becoming CEO, Rick's modus operandi did not entail aggressive risk-taking. But until 2009, he'd never been confronted with a situation where the bank's very existence might depend on his position. During those years, he had gained insight into the bank's history, its values, culture and tradition. It guided his every day activities but never posed a serious challenge. In fact, his faith and upbringing provided adequate moral and ethical infrastructure for whatever he faced. Now in 2009, the safe path was clear. There were many examples of that route being selected. The industry's vision clashed with the vision that Rick derived from his understanding of Northern Trust's historic culture.

It wasn't that the more difficult path was the right thing and the other path wasn't. There were plenty of lawyers, directors and colleagues who would have supported Rick in doing the right thing had he made the same choice that others did. It was that Rick felt the need to get more specific. Beyond what is the right thing, there was the question: what is the right thing for Northern Trust? Retro Vision answered that question for Rick, and he knew what had to be done.

Rick checked with experts, at significant cost, on how to do it legally. Rick still had to deal with those bank officers who were naysayers. While the bankers felt sorry for the clients, there really was nothing the bank could do in the naysayers' view. The Bank *had* fulfilled its fiduciary obligations. Still, Rick concluded that the bank had to do the right thing. So he decided that the bank would buy the auction rate securities.

To accomplish that, the bank had to risk over half a billion dollars, take a loss on the books, and face a huge hit on the annual bottom line. So much so that when the time came for employee bonuses, traditionally a significant part of executive compensation, Waddell decreed that none of the leadership would get bonuses. Bonuses would be paid to other employees but not to the top leaders, including, of course, Rick Waddell: no bonus for Rick either.

Some might say Waddell took this action to gain valuable PR. No doubt it did have a PR benefit with customers. But he insists PR was not his motive: "That wasn't the purpose. At the time, I thought there was more downside risk than upside."

There were some angry clients. One such client told Rick that clients only wanted to be treated fairly. That seems like a reasonable request, especially by a client to his bank, to his fiduciary. But these were extreme times. Rick tried explaining to that customer that times dictated that the bank try to be equitable. He told the client that "fair" was too subjective and nearly impossible in a world that wasn't acting in a fair manner.

Rick says, "I take great comfort in saying that we did the right thing. And I'll live with that."

As Waddell told all this to me, I was curious: what made him do this? He loved both his employer and his job. Most people take the route more likely to preserve and safeguard what they love. He, on the other hand, admittedly chose a path he believed to have "more downside risk than upside risk." That's an interesting analysis coming from a self-described optimist. Sure, he conferred with his board and especially the chairman of the board, Bill Osborn, who preceded Rick as CEO. [Waddell #3]

If things went wrong—if the chosen action did adversely affect the bank's capital, then vulture investors might well try to steal the bank at the artificially deflated value that would have resulted. In that case, Waddell's job could well have been in peril. However laudable Rick's motives, a bad result generally demands that someone pay the price.

Given the government's position—that Northern Trust misbehaved by wanting to prematurely repay the debt it neither needed nor wanted to borrow and that the good guys, the solid banks, had to pay the price for the bad guys' foibles—it wasn't likely the government would come to Rick's aid.

Indeed, the government officials likely would have taken at least some solace, if not outright joy, in whatever retribution was meted out to Waddell. They were likely in no mood to salute the purity of his motives.

Waddell's background was pretty normal. He came from a middle-class to upper-middle-class, Midwestern (Pittsburgh) family, loved sports and was a "a pretty good, not great, student, with A's and B's. We went to church every Sunday, and so all that was pretty normal."

An uncle by marriage urged Rick to apply to Dartmouth. His dad drove him out to visit for the first time. Rick fell in love with Dartmouth while the car was still moving and he first saw the campus from the top of a hill.

That was just after the road crossed the Connecticut River passing from Vermont to New Hampshire. Despite his early concerns about getting in, clearly he was well-suited for Dartmouth. He was accepted. He did well scholastically and became president of his fraternity.

In considering what to do after Dartmouth, he thought about law school. But law school would have put a financial burden on his parents and necessitate him incurring debt. [Waddell #4]

So instead, he decided to find a job. He participated in the school's on-campus recruiting program. Ultimately, he rejected an offer from Fidelity National Bank of Newark, New Jersey. He accepted a somewhat less generous offer from Northern Trust. He'd never even heard of Northern Trust, but he was quite impressed by the interviews (seven or eight as he recalls).

When Rick talks about his favorite of those interviews at Northern Trust, he refers to one on campus by E. Leroy Hall, the chief administrative officer who worked for Mr. Smith, then Northern Trust's CEO and a member of the family that founded the bank in 1889.

Instead of the customary, "we'll get back to you," Hall said, "if you would like to know more about Northern Trust, write me a letter." Impressed, Rick wrote. And he took the job Northern Trust was to offer him.

But Rick's favorite interview at Northern Trust actually occurred in 1987, a dozen years after he chose the bank.

That one was with Wes Christopherson, then Chairman and CEO of Northern Trust. Christopherson had asked Waddell to be the bank's Strategic Planning Officer, which Rick was excited about. When Rick asked Wes what the job expectations were, he asked Rick to draw the organization chart of the bank. Rick started drawing the typical chart—CEO at the top, lines down to vice presidents, further lines down to assistant vice presidents, and so on.

Christopherson told Rick to turn the chart upside down. He then said that Rick had had it backwards, because the top of the chart should be clients, that "the people who run the place are the clients; the people who are next most important are the people who deal with the clients." Wes went on to say, "I work for you, and when you figure out what you want me to do, then we'll have this conversation." Waddell says "that was a paradigm shift moment for me." [Waddell #5]

Of course, it's no surprise Rick reacted so positively. Some might have left that meeting thinking that the CEO was less than helpful, refusing to answer the question, leaving his junior officer confused. But Waddell had already fallen in love with Northern Trust.

Northern Trust's facilities were elegant, but Rick had fallen in love with much more than tangible accoutrements.

He had fallen for the bank's values and heritage that were then over a hundred years old. Rick likely fell in love with Northern Trust almost immediately, which is no surprise, given his experience upon first seeing Dartmouth. What was surprising was that Rick didn't know he was in love with the bank.

Rick didn't get it until he was about 40 years old, when his college roommate, Bruce Williamson, shocked him with the realization. Bruce was a guy whose goal had been to become a CEO, a goal he achieved twice. They were out having a couple of beers, talking about passion in business.

Rick said, "I really don't know what I'm passionate about." To that Rick remembers Bruce replying, "Come on you don't know? You love the Northern Trust. You would do anything legal for the Northern Trust. That's all you talk about. You love it. All your friends are from the Northern Trust. You're doing a great job at the Northern Trust. They love you. You love them. It's your whole life." [Waddell #6]

Rick says, "The bank being my passion never occurred to me." In a sense, Bruce was right. Rick would say that the bank wasn't his first priority.

He lists his priorities in this order: "my faith, my family, my friends, the bank's clients, and the bank and then golf." I guess that's par for the course. [Waddell #7]

Rick says he never aspired to the position of CEO of Northern Trust and that he'd have been just fine in another job at Northern Trust. Perhaps, but being CEO allows Rick to feel responsible for and proud of the people at Northern Trust.

Rick told me a story that immediately told me he was a unique CEO and a good person. On reflection, however, it told me much more, adding another brick to the foundation underlying Rick's decision that the bank should take the hit on the customers' short-term asset illiquidity.

Whenever he didn't have a lunch meeting, Rick would go to the employee cafeteria and sit down with some employees he didn't know. In the hard times following the years 2008-2009, Northern Trust closed three branches in Chicago and people were being laid off at headquarters.

Waddell sat down with a group of three women for lunch. He introduced himself and asked each of them what she was working on. One responded that she had just received notice that she was being laid off. Rick told her how sorry he was and asked if there was anything he could do. He asked how HR was doing, whether they were helping her, and he started to explain why the layoffs were necessary. She said she understood and wound up reassuring him that everything would be okay with her. [Waddell #8]

THE VISION THING

Rick Took Bank Clients' Best Interests to Heart

I have no doubt that Rick was moved by that experience. Laying-off employees is very tough on CEOs, but most are insulated by the moat around the executive suite. Rick chose to lower the drawbridge on that moat. Rick knew how emotionally vulnerable he would be in such a situation (he admits to crying as he watches "It's a Wonderful Life"), but he willingly exposed himself to discussing layoffs directly with those suffering them.

Even when his valued employees were being laid-off, Rick had a positive attitude. When he caused the bank to take a serious charge for the loss incurred by saving the customers from trading losses, he had a positive attitude. Even when he issued an edict that none of the top executives would receive an annual bonus, which meant each of them, including Rick, would lose a serious percentage of their compensation, his attitude was positive.

He felt it important for those at the bottom of the (Wes Christopherson) organization chart to demonstrate that they were working for the clients and the other employees.

So too, when Rick made the decision that the bank, not the customers, should bear the loss, he was playing the role prescribed by the upside down chart. He would be first to take a pay cut, its top officers next, and sadly some employees were laid off, but all in an attempt to safeguard the clients. No other course of action would be consistent with Rick's love for Northern Trust and his belief in the upside-down chart.

In effect, Rick had so deeply bought into the bank's culture and values, that he had no choice. It's an extraordinary example of Retro Vision— searching back to his predecessors' values and value scheme and bringing it forward to form a basis for current action and for the future, come what may.

Much has been written about what makes great U.S. Presidents great. The very office provides a magnifying glass for the occupant's character and ability. Some say "the office makes the man [or woman]," but the ultimate lever to greatness starts with the opportunity provided by circumstances: Harry Truman, an obscure Senator from Missouri stepped into the shoes of the great Franklin Delano Roosevelt near the end of World War II.

Through Truman's steady principled leadership he emerged as a visionary and, at least, a near great president. The same can be said of business visionaries: Circumstances make visionaries.

Just as Waddell had no clue that he loved Northern Trust, Rick likely didn't know he was a business visionary, let alone a devotee of Retro Vision. When his vision led him to risk all, it was the circumstances—the plight of the bank customer—that led Retro Vision to emerge and demonstrate that he was a true visionary.

Vision Chart

(For Chapter 9)

▸ A crisis often switches focus to the immediate time frame. A crisis is best solved by maintaining focus on the business vision. The Great Recession was an existential threat to the banking industry. Yet, the best solution was for Rick to seek out Northern Trust's long-term vision.

▸ You needn't be a founder to be a business visionary. Some forge new visions for older companies, ala Wirtz, Terlato, etc., while others reach back with Retro Vision.

The Vision Transition

Bank CEOs with far more experience than Rick Waddell would say that then-current best practices would suffice. Rick felt those tools were inadequate and effectively threw them out.

Jim Stevens had less experience than most CEOs, less than his father George. Jim even had less experience than the employees assigned to his team to solve a key problem: developing a Weber gas grill. Would he pull it off?

CHAPTER 10

Jim Stephen

The Weber Story: Not Your Father's Old Grill

▼▼▼▼▼▼▼▼▼▼▼

*G*eorge Stephen invented the once ubiquitous Weber grill pieced together from a pair of black buoy halves. The charcoal burner dominated the market for decades, and sales jumped with George's growing family. But natural gas loomed on the grilling horizon, a clear threat to Weber market dominance. Could son, Jim Stephen, build a boxy gas Weber better than all others and create a dominant future to echo the past? If so, son Jim could echo his father's vision. This seemed unlikely in backyards littered with gas failures.

A Passion Heats Up

Visit an outdoor barbecue grill display and you'll find most are gas-fueled and boxy. They range in size from small portables to family-reunion-sized monsters. Also likely on site: a lone Weber kettle-shaped, charcoal grill.

Decades ago, Weber charcoal grills dominated such displays like so many domes arising out of a small cluster of rectangular charcoal grills that looked vaguely out of place. None of the Weber rivals was particularly good at broiling burgers or baking potatoes. They weren't durable either.

The Weber kettle grill was invented in 1952 by George Stephen. He worked for Weber Brothers, a fabricator of metal components for various manufacturers of finished products. One Weber product was the outer shells of buoys, those globe-shaped floating devices commonly seen near the seashore.

But first, George, who was handy, had used excess bricks from his new home in suburban Chicago to build a barbecue grill for his backyard. It looked great but was unsatisfactory. No matter how careful he was, George kept burning the food and polluting his neighborhood with clouds of black smoke.

Exasperated, it occurred to George to use parts of existing production salt water buoys to make a grill. He took two buoy halves, drilled holes for ventilation to control temperature and added a four-legged stand. Then he began experimenting with charcoal briquettes and timers. In time, the Weber grill was born. Would it be superior to the other grills on the market? [Stephen #1]

George focused on refining the process he had created with the buoy halves. His objective was constant—to build a better barbecue. His brick barbecue grill was not the right route.

Proud of his work, George showed his grill to neighbors. Impressed, they asked him to make Weber grills for them.

Clearly, his new kettle grill filled a need. But George knew that the transition from inventor to entrepreneur would be tricky.

He was indeed smart, creative and a good salesman. But he obviously lacked both knowledge and experience in the art of starting, building and scaling a business to serve his invention.

Though George was a good salesman, he was not a slick, in-your-face kind of guy. Unlike some others in the business world who allow their egos to direct their efforts, George listened to his customers' experiences with his new invention. They were delighted with this truly-effective means of back yard cooking. Because he cared about his customers and was flexible, he soon learned his four-legged stand was a problem. Customers said patios were uneven. Only three legged stands offered stability.

So he quickly switched to a three legged stand. Smart! Being out of touch with customers can bury you. But that sales technique was indicative of George's Midwest principles: value your own idea but realize that having a good idea doesn't make you smarter than your customers or your employees.

George couldn't afford a serious marketing campaign, so he stationed himself outside local hardware stores, lawn and garden centers and in parking lots. Spatula in hand and burgers on the fire, he demonstrated how to use the Weber grill and allowed spectators free tastes of the delicious results.

George Stephen, it seems, settled into a necessary but affordable marketing plan. And like the talented cooks on today's Food Channel, George combined a cooking lesson with an effective sales pitch. Forget: "Don't try this at home." George urged: "Do try this at home." And try it they did. [Stephen #2]

His manufacturer-to-consumer business model benefited from better margins by eliminating the middlemen. But George was limited to one-on-one sales, which was hardly a good model for scaling the business versus concurrent exposures. One TV spot would have been vastly superior to stand-up at someone's retail garden center.

Wait! There was also a word-of-mouth and over the backyard fence aspect. George was not the only one who was proud to show off his kettle grill. Grill owners were proud to demonstrate their new toy to their dinner guests.

According to George's son Jim, the future CEO of Weber, each customer echoed George's demonstrations: "Here's how you do direct and indirect cooking. Here's how many coals you put in each place. Here's how you put the food on. Here's how you tie a roast. Here's how you spice it. Here's when you put the lid on, and here's how long it will take to cook." And they all bragged about their new "high tech" gizmo (the use of rotating vent covers, which cost Weber next to nothing, was a "high tech" element in that low tech era that made the grill work so well).

Jim Stephen calls word of mouth the "social media of the day." The back yard show and its outcome—a better-tasting grilled meal—caused guests to buy their own grills. That created a minor leverage factor and enough volume that a few local stores started carrying the product.

Proof of Concept

George was conducting a process known as "proof of concept." He was demonstrating that there was a covert need. People were not satisfied with existing barbecue grills but not realizing that there was a better alternative, they remained passively in need.

Despite being superior, the odd-shaped device was anything but self-explanatory. Customers not only required lessons to use it effectively; they even needed to be told that the device was a barbecue grill. Upon witnessing the Weber Grill in use, their passive need became active demand. They were quite willing to pay the price and take the time to learn how to use it.

Although based on a limited population survey—following an agonizingly slow process—this informal test was proof of concept. However, the distance between proof of concept and commercial success was enormous. To get broad demand required broadly demonstrated usage. Sure, it could have been shown on TV. But that was expensive, and prospects couldn't taste the delicious food.

George continued selling the kettle grill through Weber Brothers, improving his pitch and increasing the number of demonstrations he conducted. The combination of one-on-one sales, both through demonstrations and by word-of-mouth, was growing. The grill business showed promise and potential, but growth was slow. George knew scaling needed more focus.

Fortuitously, the owners of the business for which George still worked, the Weber brothers wished to retire. They agreed to sell control of their company to George, who could run the business. The Webers also sold a minority share to Harold White, an unrelated investor who provided necessary capital for the brothers' retirements.

When George urged the company to get out of the component business and focus on grills, the investor suggested splitting the business. George agreed. White kept the component business. George kept the grill business with some equipment to continue making grills.

George had the vision to give up the heart of the business, risking disaster. In doing so, George was making a giant leap. The grill business was still in the startup phase, without evidence that scaling was realistic for it. Thus, George was demonstrating astounding confidence. George was simply convinced that his customers loved his product, so why wouldn't millions of others love it. As to scaling, George was satisfied with incremental growth. He wasn't bothered by what he didn't know—kind of "what you don't know can't hurt you." [Stephen #3]

Believing he had built a recognized brand, George kept the Weber name and called his new company, Weber Stephen Products Co. It was at best a local brand, but George's vision was one of incrementally expanding local growth. He'd simply drive to the next city, where he would do the same watch-and-taste demonstrations, and then to the next city and so on.

Today's New Product Dilemma: Timing vs. Quality

George's proof of concept took an inordinately long time. Even when he made his move to market, growth was at a pace that, today, would be unacceptably slow. That Weber succeeded despite those delays can be attributed to three factors. First, competitors ignored the kettle grill. They assumed it was a fad. So they focused on other prospects. Second, the world simply moved more slowly then. Third, George obtained patent protection. His patent was strong and posed a significant barrier to competition, affording him the luxury of decades to grow.

The luxury of time that facilitated George's progress, no longer exists; the clock is less forgiving today. Current entrepreneurs face a unique dilemma: timing vs. quality.

Back then, many would forego the first-to-market option that gave the first out a boost. They feared they'd never live down initial poor quality, an almost inevitable result of haste.

Today, entrepreneurs are urged to move quickly. Indeed, some opt to send goods to market *despite obvious flaws*. They hope that customer feedback and easy return policies can enable them to have first-to-market advantage and, after fixes, superior products.

That approach likely would have proved abhorrent to George Stephen who was a perfectionist. Fortunately, he wasn't burdened with today's time sensitivities. The New Tradition Is Replacement, Not Repair.

Patent Defense is Patently Absurd

Patent protection is still valuable to entrepreneurs. But these days, a patent is only as strong as the owner's financial ability to litigate.

The cost of litigation, including appeals, has become staggering, even in the tens of millions of dollars in landmark cases. And the time of litigation, often years, is a time of uncertainty. Investors and other stakeholders abhor uncertainty, especially the patent litigation kind of uncertainty. Patent litigators lack a crystal ball. During pendency, surviving, let alone scaling, can be a treacherous, unaffordable challenge.

Though product distribution gains were slow, George's process worked. George's new company hired a couple of salesmen who conducted their own outdoor demos and made sales calls on stores that were becoming impressed with the parking lot sales results. By the mid-1970s, sales were growing—albeit still incrementally—and the business was expanding. Weber's creeping sales gains might have satisfied some. As for George, he was satisfied making enough to support himself and his family. But what a family! George had twelve children. His mind set was that all of them would come to work with him. In fact, all but one of his children *did* join the family business.

To George family was number one. As long as he could continue to grow the business sufficiently to absorb his kids, life was good. Happily, he had instilled the Stephen family values. His values dictated a modest style of living in all his kids. So, incremental growth sufficed for a time. But the kids got married and had children of their own. Clearly, the family expansion was exceeding the company's incremental growth. Something more was needed if all the new mouths were to be fed by the family business.

For George, that meant selling more and more kettle grills. But perhaps he needed a second product too.

Around the mid-'70s, other manufacturers were focusing on grills fueled by gas. Some, like Charm Glow, were promoted by large natural gas companies that saw the ploy as a means of increasing gas consumption.

By then, Weber had gained virtual iconic status. Customers no longer needed explanations of what the globe shaped device did. Indeed, if someone said "Weber," the Weber barbecue grill came to mind. Even the silhouette of the kettle grill was recognized as a Weber grill.

Of course Weber Stephen Products did not operate in a vacuum. The advent of competitors' gas grills could not be ignored. If successful, gas grills could slow Weber's incremental growth and preclude exponential growth. That would deflate George's long term dream for his family.

Everyone on the executive team at Weber wanted to have a second product. His son Jim Stephen recalls that they were often asked, "What else do you make?" When they'd respond, "All we make is barbecues," people were incredulous. He recalls that his dad would lie in bed at night wondering, "Geez, how many barbecues can I sell? When does this thing stop? When does somebody come up with something better, leaving me tottering as I have only one leg to stand on?" He was not oblivious to the obvious: He knew that Weber status quo could bury the firm.

That approach, even more than entrepreneurial thinking, prompted Weber's key employees to make several attempts at new product lines. Their customers at that time were largely new home owners. That was not because they were the only people buying a new kind of barbecue but because our nation was fueling its largest boom in new home ownership.

Being motivated was only half the solution. For key employees to risk position in the company, there had to be an atmosphere conducive to risk. That existed at Weber but not by happenstance.

George Stephen was known as an inventor and salesman. However, he was also a business leader. His leadership style reflected his understanding of himself. He knew what he was good at and understood where he fell short of what was needed.

So he established policies: Hire the best possible people whose skills complemented his and give them latitude to try things and to make mistakes. He didn't, however, give them blank checks. They were keenly aware of the limitations: they couldn't bet the farm, of course. And at certain points they had to convince George of the validity of their efforts.

Various Weber executives experimented with mail boxes, bird feeders—and even the bird seed to fill them, all under the Weber brand. Bird seed? Give us a break! It almost sounds like a school class with a substitute teacher. The phrase, "the inmates have taken over the asylum," comes to mind. Wrong. In fact, this was the special entrepreneurial atmosphere that George favored.

He always said he succeeded because he hired the best talent and let them do their thing. Well, you can't just say it; you must also let the talent do it. And that is what George did.

He let his key people try whatever they thought might work. It would have been great if the first attempt resulted in another great success. But that also would have been surprising. Even so, bird seed aside, George would not have referred to the mail box and bird feeder efforts as failures, per se.

Those efforts were the price George paid to establish an atmosphere where people tested their creative ideas. He was confident that somewhere along the line, they would come up with something great: a highly-marketable second product that would carry Weber into its next era of prosperity.

Yet George was ever watchful, ever cautious. As Jim said, "He wouldn't allow us to make a killer mistake." Jim believes that knowing that his dad could pull the plug on any project at any time, combined with George's high quality standards, motivated the Weber teams to work harder.

That approach worked. Eventually, Weber developed a very important second product that ultimately succeeded, but not without false starts. In one clever try, George's eldest son, George Jr., converted a Weber kettle grill into a gas grill.

George Jr. fitted his version of the kettle grill with a burner that was raised and lowered to adjust the heat. On the outside, it looked like any Weber kettle barbecue. It had simply been outfitted with a gas jet inside the kettle. Close but no cigar.

Some readers might be thinking—"Big deal! Allowing George Jr. to make that foray was just a father letting his son play with his toy." But that's an inaccurate read. George, Sr. had rules, which he applied equally to all executives, family or not.

Despite George's desire to hire all his kids to work at Weber, everyone knew that his kids had to toe the mark at Weber the same as everyone else at the company. Today that is generally prevailing wisdom at all successful family businesses—best practice if you will. George, Sr., was ahead of his time.

In the meantime, George Sr. was trying to get his son, Jim, to move back from California, where Jim had been pursuing an acting career. Jim agreed to come to work at Weber, if he could be the salesman for any new gas grill. [Stephen #4] Jim saw others' gas grills as a real threat. True, the resulting food didn't taste as good and the grills were nowhere near as durable. But gas grills were so much easier and more convenient. There was no pouring of briquettes with the plume of charcoal dust in your face, no layering the coals in different configurations for different foods. There was no adjusting and readjusting the ventilation holes.

Best of all, there was no weary trip to the back yard late at night to scrape the residue off the grill after the ashes cooled. Jim realized the novelty and quality of the Weber kettle grill might be outweighed by the weariness of the consumers.

Generally, there was a growing belief that gas grills might someday put most charcoal barbecues on the scrap heap.

Jim realized that his brother's gas-fueled Weber *kettle* grill had two problems. First, it was a good barbecue, but was not a great one. Engineering and tooling flaws led to uneven cooking. True, those flaws reflected cautionary budget restrictions. But secondly and according to Jim, "It was an impossible sell."

Customers would look at the gas barbecue. What they would "see" was Weber's charcoal fueled kettle which they knew and recognized so well. Jim would do the same kind of demonstrations his father had done, showing how to use the grill and extolling its virtues. But at least one customer, who had watched Jim demonstrate the gas grill, actually said, "Yeah, but Weber doesn't make gas barbecues." And Jim had just finished telling him that it was a *Weber Gas Barbeque.* [Stephen #5]

That was interesting, but shouldn't have been a surprise. It showed that Weber was identified with charcoal kettle barbecues only. More importantly, it made clear that gas grills were assumed to be rectangular in shape and to have a hinged top.

In the meantime, there was growing belief that, in the future, barbecuing with charcoal would not be as popular as it had been.

Jim had learned how and when to approach his father with new ideas. It wasn't that Jim considered his father intimidating. Indeed, George, Sr. was a patient mentor for all of his kids.

Jim knew his father was a perfectionist and Jim remembered his dad's brick barbecue. It wasn't simply that George was a perfectionist. He did good homework and learned from mistakes, his own and those of others. He kept his eye on the goal. Minor setbacks would justify yet another redo.

The goal, indeed his vision, was market dominance. He never varied. And he expected his kids and his employees to reflect seriously on consequences before offering him important decisions.

So Jim picked Mike Hempster, an esteemed Weber staffer to accompany him when he would urge his dad to consider developing a rectangular, hinged top, gas fueled grill.

(Interestingly, going from globe to a rectangular shape was effectively learning to grill within the box, a different kind of challenge for an entrepreneur who thinks outside the box.)

Jim had no clear evidence as to how the market would shake out. He was only 28 and had no real experience in the field. But he had picked an ally his father respected. Besides, Jim was fully confident and of one thing he was certain—Weber had to be positioned in case gas became dominant. If anyone was going to "knock off Weber's grill it should be Weber."

Or in the more modern vernacular, if anyone was to eat Weber's lunch—or should we say "cook Weber's lunch"—it should be a Weber-quality gas-fired grill. His father agreed that Jim and Mike should push ahead with this risky endeavor.

Let's be clear on this. Weber had the best products, was building market share, and appeared destined to continue to dominate the *charcoal* fueled grill market. Moreover, market for gas grills was growing slowly. So far, box grills lacked quality, dependability and durability. Worse yet, they made inferior tasting food. Granted, some had the sponsorship of big natural gas companies, but even with that plus they weren't making great inroads. (Utilities, often monopolies, were not really creative with the basics: serving consumers' energy needs.)

In short, the future of gas grills was anything but certain. Clearly, the cards were not stacked in Jim's favor.

Weber was not flush with cash. Serious money would be diverted to developing, manufacturing, and marketing gas grills. There would be less money left to grow the kettle grill business.

Corporate graveyards are filled with companies that digressed from existing business to follow a siren song. Focus is the unassailable mantra in business, as in other pursuits. Avoiding attractive distractions is not rocket science.

A decision to pursue gas grills could stall or even torpedo the drive to grow the kettle grill business. Yes, Jim was taking a big gamble. If he chose to concentrate on gas grills, he might snuff his father's dream. If he didn't take the gamble and a rival won a gas grill race – the outcome would be grim, even fatal.

That was a lot for the prodigal son to take on. Yet Jim was not overwhelmed about taking on such a risky project.

▼▼▼▼▼▼▼▼▼▼▼▼▼▼▼▼▼▼▼▼▼▼▼▼▼▼▼▼▼▼▼

Finding a Trustworthy Assistant and Mentor

Jim realized he was too new to the field to do this alone. He needed guidance from someone with experience, someone who understood the industry and also Weber Stephen.

While Jim understood George's rules as a father (and as boat captain from their frequent sailings together), Jim was new to Weber as an employee. He needed someone who understood how all that was applied at Weber. He needed someone who knew the standard limits of the box's perimeter but also how to transcend those boundaries. That's why he enlisted Mike Hempster. Mike could provide all that. Importantly, Mike's opinion would be unwaveringly trusted by Jim's father, George.

Obviously, Mike was a good choice, since Jim later described Mike as the "best businessman he ever knew."

▲▲▲▲▲▲▲▲▲▲▲▲▲▲▲▲▲▲▲▲▲▲▲▲▲▲▲▲▲▲▲

Mike Hempster joined Jim and together corralled a team of employees, started investigating the competitors' products—buying and reverse engineering all that was out there. They learned that the competitors had copied each other. Each had a lava rock inside. What's more, they were all cheaply made. Worse still, they did not work very well.

Jim soon realized the process was taking far too long, and was failing to yield any meaningful progress. Try as they may, they knew they weren't near coming up with something good enough to present to George Sr. Finally, Jim realized that his vision: copying competitors' approaches for a gas grill conflicted with his father's vision for highest quality grills. So he walked into the shop and told the staff to trash all of the competitors' products. [Stephen #6]

Jim Stephen's Answer to Schlock: Don't Imitate; Innovate

"You know what," Jim said, "let's throw all these out. Let's get rid of them. I want them all out of here." He brought in his dad's kettle barbecue: "This is the quality standard we're going for. Because nothing cooks better than dad's barbecue. Nothing has better flare control. Nothing times the cooking better."

This changed the focus of the quest for a superior product. None of the competitors' products would meet George's standards. So it was illogical to base a new Weber grill on what they learned by reverse engineering competitors' inferior grills. This would not result in something they could show to George Sr. They would start fresh, using their own standards and skills.

▼▼▼▼▼▼▼▼▼▼▼▼▼▼▼▼▼▼▼▼▼▼▼▼▼▼▼▼▼▼

It Wasn't What They Saw but Whose Eyes They Saw It Through

Picture a mailbox, a birdfeeder and a barbecue grill. This might lead to asking, in *Sesame Street* style, "which of these is not like the others?" After Weber's executive team developed the mailbox and birdfeeder, they soon realized their efforts should be suspended.

Yet when new team leader Jim was confronted with an inability to make a high-quality gas grill through reverse engineering, Jim didn't suspend. Instead the team changed direction and continued to successful completion. Why? What was different? What did this team see?

The mailbox and birdfeeder were conceived by the other Weber executive team through their own creativity. They assumed those products, bearing a Weber brand, would appeal to Weber's loyal customers. It was an attempt at cross-selling new products to old customers. That was their vision.

The gas grill was an example of different Weber executives sensing customers' needs and working to fill that need. In other words, it was the Beyond-the-Eaves Vision at Weber.

Customers soon made it clear that a Weber mailbox and birdfeeder were not something they would buy: Demand was lacking.

Weber listened to the customers and acted contrary to Weber's "most recent decision," extraordinary [upbeat] action according to the teachings of Nobel Laureate, Daniel Kahneman.

They abandoned the unwanted products work. The team's decision to reorient the old gas grill project was based on their recognition that a significant number of customers not only would want gas grills but valued Weber's brand for the quality of its existing iconic grills. Transferring brand recognition amongst different grills would be much easier than from grills to birdfeeders or other unrelated products.

It took a long time for Weber to develop its gas grill. First, they determined that the demand was real. After all, if people were willing to buy bad gas grills, when they could have had a superior Weber *charcoal* grill, they must really want gas grills.

Then by trial and error and by chucking it all and starting over, they worked on improving quality, an important differentiator leading to a superior product.

Quality improvement wasn't a one-time event. It had to be ongoing, because competitors were soon to be reverse engineering the outstanding rectangular Weber gas grill.

Surely, there remained doubters. Some said, "It's too boxy to be a Weber," and there was the perennial "Weber doesn't make gas grills." So increased marketing became crucial.

▲▲▲▲▲▲▲▲▲▲▲▲▲▲▲▲▲▲▲▲▲▲▲▲▲▲▲▲▲▲▲

Every step an uphill battle, the challenge was met by smart homework, inspired thinking, very hard work, and a willingness to "bet on your own horse" by allocating funds and people that were needed elsewhere. None of that would have been possible without the atmosphere that encouraged employees to follow their educated instincts, to take chances, and to try new things.

They knew the limits—and they knew that George Sr. had high standards and, of course, his controlling vote. They also knew that George was absolutely committed to having the best barbecue product in whatever configuration—always.

THE VISION THING
Prepare Long and Hard To Be an Overnight Success

George Stephen led by instinct and common sense. He gave people an atmosphere that let them breathe. The key: This is not a just-in-time management procedure. This is leadership, not management. Leadership entails building an atmospheric chamber, not teaching the occupants how to breathe. If the chamber is built well in advance of its need, the occupants will breathe far better on their own than you can teach them.

In 2010, the Stephen family sold control of Weber-Stephen Co. Even if Jim Stephen were still CEO, he no longer would have been confronted with complaints that "Weber doesn't make gas barbecues." They certainly entered the gas barbecue business successfully under Jim's leadership. Still, the company continues to make charcoal barbecues, both the original kettle model and new models such as the Weber Performer Deluxe Charcoal Grill, which houses a kettle grill at one end of its rectangular chassis. Thinking inside the box still thrives.

Vision Chart

(For Chapter 10)

▶ Your original vision may need updating, as technology and social behavior change. George's vision—everyone using his kettle barbecue—became worrisome, as gas barbecues became popular.

▶ Original or earlier visions often consist of multiple vision components. George's version also involved a quality component. Jim recognized that and developed a gas barbecue that embodied George's quality standards.

The Vision Transition

Jim Stephen threw out all the new approaches to developing a gas barbecue. Instead, he went back to basics: the quality of his father's invention. David Bigelow steadfastly rejected his founder-mother's plan to expand into supermarkets. That came later—a result of Ruth's vision and determination.

CHAPTER 11

Ruth Bigelow

Ruth Bigelow's Pride: Spicy Tempest in a Tea Pot

▼▼▼▼▼▼▼▼▼▼▼▼▼

*C*onstant Comment Tea, an exotic blend of tea and spices, was found in gift shops. But Ruth Bigelow wanted her popular Bigelow Teas to attract more consumers in supermarkets where Lipton's black tea was the dominant brand. Could Ruth's tea, costing five times Lipton's, hit that mark? Ruth founded Bigelow Tea in 1945. A generation passed, and Bigelow had grown to have everything to lose before her gamble was tried.

Pick on Someone Your Own Size

This is the story of Bigelow Tea and the firm's Constant Comment brand, both created by founder Ruth Bigelow. Ruth's vision: Americans choosing exotic teas instead of the overwhelming market leader, Lipton. Ruth's tea cost five times as much as Lipton's traditional black tea which was so dominant that other tea brands didn't appear on grocery and supermarket tea shelves when Ruth set up her petite company in 1945.

Yet, Ruth Bigelow believed her aromatic orange and spice flavored Constant Comment Tea would thrive if given shelf space next to Lipton's.

It was the only path to the mass market. This could achieve Ruth's dream of Americans choosing her tea, while bringing her superior returns. This also entailed enormous risks, so much so that everyone advised against it. It's usually the big bully who is admonished to "pick on someone your own size."

Ruth was a 5-foot 4-inch dynamo. Charming and fun to be with—she was versed in many topics and, of course, inventive: also determined—like her granddaughter, as Cindi's dad explained.

Yet Ruth Bigelow, a Connecticut homemaker, was warned, even cajoled, not to pick on the industry giant, Lipton. It was as though they feared she'd be trashed like a used tea bag. But before this risky vision was set in motion, Bigelow progressed as a low volume novelty in the nation's gift stores where scalability—the key to commercial grandeur—was severely limited.

Ruth's son David, who in 1963 followed as CEO, had more fear about the consequences of changing channels of distribution than faith in his mother's big store vision. Bigelow grew and was profitable under David. But the business wasn't fully scalable. Ruth's vision was undoable while they sold through gift stores.

David eventually acceded to his mother's wishes. Despite the odds, Bigelow's success proved: Mother knew best.

Ruth's granddaughter, Cindi, two generations removed from the inspired idea but smart, energetic and committed was to reap the plus of supermarket sales and achieve Ruth's vision. Cindi had replaced her dad, David, as CEO in 2006. Ruth didn't live to see Cindi's accession.

Ruth's plan to carve out space for her tea in the nation's supermarkets meant a war where the first battle was with broadcast's reigning icon.

Lipton Tea sponsored an entertainment phenomenon in Arthur Godfrey, a humorist with on-air shows, who sang along as he plunked a ukulele on daytime radio and later on prime time TV, all the while sipping Lipton's and touting it to listeners.

Godfrey dominated the broadcast world for CBS with his daytime radio show and five prime time half hours on TV to reach 80 million people each week in the early 1950s.

Yet the magic in this story is that founder Ruth Bigelow was not daunted by the odds of competing directly with a company so entrenched that even her family opposed her. After all, she had a vision.

Ruth Bigelow and the Genesis of a Hot Idea

Some years after Ruth Bigelow and her husband lost everything during the Great Depression, Ruth started her new tea business in the kitchen with her husband's support. She did not like the plain black tea made by Lipton. But that was pretty much all you could buy at the A&P or at the mom and pop grocery stores that were situated every few blocks in cities back then. So when she had friends over, she brewed her own tea—blending orange peel and selected spices with black tea. Friends told Ruth that her tea was so good, so unique that it generated "constant comment." And so, when she decided to package and sell her blend of tea, she named it "Constant Comment." [Bigelow #1]

That was 72 years ago, and the name has stuck. That item continues to be the biggest seller for the now $150 million company which features exotic teas for every taste.

▼▼▼▼▼▼▼▼▼▼▼▼▼▼▼▼▼▼▼▼▼▼▼▼▼▼▼▼▼▼▼▼

What's In a Name?

Some companies pay experts huge fees to find names for new products. Often, the right name is right under your nose or your friends' noses, as it was for Constant Comment.

Of course, if you do sniff out your own name, do get expert help to be sure the name is legally available, not trademarked by another. Then take steps to protect it for your own use.

▲▲▲▲▲▲▲▲▲▲▲▲▲▲▲▲▲▲▲▲▲▲▲▲▲▲▲▲▲▲▲▲▲▲▲

That Constant Comment still leads in sales decades after the company's start belies Bigelow's tortuous road to stardom.

Selling a new product is never easy. Ruth couldn't afford to market to consumers. Even if she could have, it would have cost a ton. Lipton was by far the number one tea in America.

In addition to Lipton's massive budget for print media ads, the company sponsored the most popular radio show in the country: *Arthur Godfrey and His Friends.* Its star, Arthur Godfrey, was known for talking to the audience, periodically strumming his ukulele and almost always sipping and commenting favorably on his cup of Lipton tea.

It was the ultimate combination of endorsement and product placement. In such placements, an actor might be shown nonchalantly reaching for a Coca Cola or 007 driving an Aston Martin without even mentioning the brand. Companies pay handsomely to have their product used in a show or in a movie. The subliminal effect is immense.

However, this was even better: it was combined with an outright, continual endorsement. There was not much subtlety with Arthur Godfrey. His continual endorsement of the product in his soft, nasal, baritone, would have been akin to Michael Jordan endorsing Nike shoes by wearing them in every game and pointing to the swoosh logo after every good play.

Ruth Bigelow had to do it the old-fashioned way—at first going to local grocery stores and pleading with the proprietor to leave a jar of her Constant Comment on the counter.

Back then, grocery stores were not self-service. Customers would go to the counter and give the grocer a handwritten list. He would gather the items and bring them to the counter where the customer paid cash. (There were no credit cards then, and grocers rarely carried clients *on the cuff*, an expression which may relate to a time when bartenders kept drinker's tabs on their shirt cuffs.)

Ruth hoped that customers might be curious enough to buy a jar. There were, however, no takers. The story goes: she went to a grocery store in Ridgefield, Connecticut near her home. The grocer told Ruth that he experienced no demand for the product, so he had no reason to carry it.

A customer overheard the conversation and asked Ruth about the product. Ruth's son, David Bigelow's second CEO, says: "This was a very defining moment in our history, because my mother took the glass jar, which had a screw cap on it, opened it up and let the lady take a whiff of the tea. And a whiff of Constant Comment made a huge difference, because it has this orange and spice aroma. So the lady immediately bought a jar right there on the spot." The grocer took all six jars that Ruth had brought with her. When she came back they were all gone.

The same customer had come back and bought all six jars. So Ruth started leaving whiffing jars next to the sealed jars of Constant Comment, so customers could be sold by the whiff of orange peel and spices and buy the tea. [Bigelow #2]

Ruth's husband's friend, a broker in the food business, urged the Bigelows to shun the grocery store market and focus instead on gift stores. Son David refers to that as "the big break." Indeed, it did open a channel of distribution: all those little gift stores that existed in so many small towns and big cities across America. That channel seemed appropriate— given Constant Comment's higher price, unique flavor and better quality. [Bigelow #3]

By then they had changed from glass jars to pretty hand painted cans that were more gift-worthy. Besides, cracking the grocery store market had seemed quite difficult, so when the broker friend argued that grocery stores were inappropriate for Constant Comment, it was rather easy to opt to sell to gift shops.

At least it was easy for Ruth's husband. Ruth also consented to the easier path. But given all that happened then and later, I can't help but feel that, deep down, Ruth was less enthusiastic than her mate about giving up on grocery stores.

Ruth had a clear vision not unlike Tony Terlato's (they did not know each other). She saw Americans breaking their Lipton habit, the equivalent of buying indistinguishable bulk wines, and switching to a unique, aromatic, blended tea, namely Constant Comment. An element of this was her vision of an eventual trend. Trend Pattern Vision is the ability to grasp what is likely to happen, ala Terlato.

She saw that tons of Lipton tea had been sold in grocery stores. That's where people went to buy tea. [Bigelow #4] Yes, grocery store shelves had only Lipton tea, and Lipton "owned" considerable shelf space. That in itself was amazing considering that this was tea in a country that drank coffee as its basic hot drink staple.

Only water was drunk in America in greater quantities than coffee: coffee had shelf space many times that of tea. There were numerous coffee brands to accommodate consumers' overwhelming preference for coffee.

During the World War II years, coffee and tea were less available, since neither was grown in the United States at the time. Besides, ships were focused on military-related cargo. So the end of the war might have been a perfect opportunity to switch America's taste from coffee to tea.

Lipton lacked the capacity to compete with coffee.

But Constant Comment was just getting started then. It was too expensive for Americans who had limited income and a Depression era mentality.

The gift stores proved a good outlet but not a great one. David, Ruth's son, told me that at the peak, they were selling to 12,000 gift stores. That may sound very good, and indeed it was a serious accomplishment, of which the Bigelows were prideful. [Bigelow #5]

It just wasn't an efficient channel of distribution. Gift stores were small and carried few of any particular item. Marketing and shipping to, and collecting from so many small stores was expensive and yielded unimpressive aggregate revenue.

Those gift stores were even smaller than the Ridgefield, Connecticut grocery where Ruth had started. Her vision of Americans drinking Constant Comment just wasn't keeping up.

After all, these were the "baby boomer" years. Not only was the population growing, it was changing demographically. People were moving from small towns into the big cities. Thereafter, they moved from the big cities to the suburbs.

Suburban sprawl was enabled by an America "with a car in every garage." (President Herbert Hoover was elected in 1928 with a motto: "A chicken in every pot, a car in every garage.") No longer were women walking to small neighborhood grocery stores where grocers checked lists and gathered purchases.

In those days, grocery markets were limited by how far women could walk carrying brown paper grocery bags without handles and wearing one inch heels. (Nike and New Balance did not yet exist. Indeed, today's informal sneakers and jeans look might have been deemed unseemly then for going shopping.)

The larger supermarkets weren't bound by women's walking limitations. Market distance was measured in miles, not blocks. That justified these much larger stores carrying greater quantities of merchandise—more SKUs and more of each SKU. As you probably know SKUs were and are stock keeping Units.

▼▼▼▼▼▼▼▼▼▼▼▼▼▼▼▼▼▼▼▼▼▼▼▼▼▼▼▼▼▼▼

The Curse of Bigness for the Specialty Producer

The supermarket philosophy of manufactures was: show a large quantity of a product. That made it more noticeable—easier to get the customers' attention. Quantity also lent credibility to the product. Customers assumed there was a big quantity because so many other customers liked the item. Seeing that reasoning by manufactures drove groceries to charge premiums for choice locations and large expanses of shelf space. Sure, that raised manufactures' costs, but it also kept smaller manufactures—and the likes of Bigelow—out of contention.

That's the atmosphere that confronted Bigelow. Literally the only tea sold in the supermarkets back then was Lipton's. They had huge shelf space, they had Arthur Godfrey, and they were the only tea known by 90 percent of Americans. Even if Bigelow could elbow its way into a supermarket, the small shelf space it might get, teeny in comparison to Lipton's, would lack attention-getting capacity. Experts predicted an inevitable outcome: abysmal failure at gaining credibility-by-volume.

Yet consumers were in supermarkets much more than in gift shops. They were starting to learn about Constant Comment and were asking for it *in* supermarkets. The supermarkets were sensitive to customers' desires and started writing and calling Bigelow asking for price lists. Nonetheless, everyone had told Ruth to stay away from grocery stores, and now supermarkets.

Son David had not been involved in the business earlier. He had been living and working in California when his father died. He came back to Bigelow Tea then, at Ruth's request. Taking over as CEO, David grew the company's business. He was proud of his accomplishment: growing the number of gift store outlets to over 12,000. He was willing to work hard to maintain, and build, the number of gift stores with *Constant Comment*.

If they moved into supermarkets, they would face two major risks. First, by being in supermarkets, they would very likely lose the gift stores. Not only would gift stores react to competition—until then, each shop had been the only outlet in town to carry *Constant Comment*—they wouldn't carry a product that lost its panache sitting on shelves that abutted Lipton tea. Lipton's was viewed as a commodity brand.

The probable result was that *Constant Comment* would lose all or virtually all its outlets—decades of hard work down the drain like leftover tea. In short, this was no tempest in a teapot. It was a bet-the-company proposition.

The second risk Bigelow would face was not making it in the supermarkets. The move would entail huge effort and not insignificant expense—actually huge expense for Bigelow.

Then they would wind up with tiny shelf space for an unknown product priced at multiples of Lipton's, with their large shelf space overwhelming Constant Comment's sliver.

Worse: the supermarket aisles had life-size pictures of Arthur Godfrey, promoting Lipton. And there was no room for a whiffing jar.

The double-whammy risk of losing the existing channel of distribution and failing to gain traction in the supermarket was a doomsday scenario. The expense in both time and money and the risk meant this approach was steeped in failure. Ruth's vision was at odds with the visions of her son and all the experts. All those with a say chose not to follow that path. Well, almost everyone.

Ruth Bigelow's Road Less Traveled

You see, Ruth still had that vision: Americans choosing Constant Comment over Lipton. She saw that achieving that goal was impossible, surely in her lifetime, if the company remained dedicated to a constricting channel of distribution: small gift stores. She understood the risks. But as is true of many successful business visionaries, her analysis was not just a "risk/reward" analysis. Risk/reward decisions were purely quantitative. Ruth's vision was also quantitative—more Americans drinking her tea—but just not purely so.

Her vision contained a key qualitative element. That reoriented her to Robert Frost's "road less traveled," or totally untraveled in Bigelow's case. For Ruth, the leap of faith then became an overwhelming force: the only route to possibly achieving her vision was by storming the supermarket category.

David told me that Ruth was adamant: she wanted to be in grocery stores right next to Lipton. David would argue: "Why do you want to be right next to Lipton? You are five times as expensive as Lipton and you're unknown."

Ruth's response: "Because that's where everybody is buying tea. They'll walk toward Lipton tea, and if you're right next to Lipton tea, you're going to get noticed."

Ruth's reasoning resembled the old adage about being misquoted in the newspapers: "Never mind good or bad, Just spell my name right." Ruth didn't care about comparisons of shelf space or price, so long as her product was visible.

Ruth kept her finger on the pulse of her customers. She exhibited a kind of Beyond-the-Eaves Vision that informed her of reactions to *Constant Comment* and *Lipton* teas. Years earlier, that vision told her not to push for a move to grocery stores and supermarkets.

Trend Pattern Vision told her things had changed. The market had become increasingly appreciative of and more willing to pay for taste and quality. This time she felt the world was different and would be more receptive to *Constant Comment*. It was time to move Bigelow tea to supermarkets.

That likely wasn't consistent with the merchandising experts' then-prevailing opinion, but then those experts didn't have Ruth's vision. They were still doing the risk/reward analysis and not focusing on this being the only route to realizing the vision.

The first risk proved accurate almost immediately. The gift stores dropped Bigelow. To them, Bigelow had become yesterday's used tea bag. But Bigelow wasn't taking chances on the second risk. They weren't relying on the "build it and they will come" notion, a flawed notion everywhere but in fantasy books and movies.

Bigelow was fortunate to obtain its own radio and TV personality, Art Linkletter, whose shows, "People Are Funny" and "Kids Say the Darndest Things," were extremely popular. One day, more or less in passing, he mentioned Constant Comment on his show. They flew out to thank and meet Linkletter, who continued mentioning their tea on the air. Unlike Godfrey who was promoting a sponsor, Linkletter simply liked the product and the people behind it. Bigelow used his picture on their point-of-sale displays, even though without Linkletter's express permission. [Bigelow #6]

Kids and Yogi Say the Darndest Things

In those days some entertainers were less territorial and ignored such usage. A friend asked Yogi Berra, decades ago, if he was paid by the Yogi Bear people who used the baseball Hall Of Fame player as a model for the highly commercial cartoon. He seemed baffled and said he had never heard from them.

New packaging was another way Bigelow distinguished its product, especially as their lines grew to numerous flavors, although *Constant Comment* remained far and away their biggest seller.

There were challenges—competition, court fights, branding experts, packaging equipment, costs, tea getting stale on the shelves, internal packaging for maintaining freshness—but the guiding principle was Ruth's vision.

Ruth Bigelow passed away in 1996. She lived to see her vision starting to take hold. In 2006, David stepped down as CEO, replaced by his daughter Cindi. [Bigelow #7] Cindi shared Ruth's vision for Bigelow, which necessitated new strategies given changes in the marketplace. For example, 85 percent of Americans' tea is iced tea. Growing Bigelow's share of that market is critical if Ruth's vision is to be sustained, but it is very challenging.

They recently launched a cold brew iced tea. It was better than the competition's, which would have satisfied most marketing experts. But Cindi determined it was not "an exceptional product," a benchmark Bigelow lives by. So she "pushed, pushed, pushed, pushed, pushed the envelope, until we actually came up with a cold brew that is very, very good."

Cindi is extraordinarily dedicated to her extremely loyal employees, to maintaining product quality, to giving back to the community, and to sustaining the environment, all while building and expanding the market for Bigelow teas. She added seasonal teas and healthy teas (lemon ginger with probiotics). [Bigelow #8]

While Ruth did not talk in terms of devotion to quality, it was simply ingrained in her single product. Cindi has similar devotion [Bigelow #9] but has different challenges insofar as she maintains Ruth's vision to get Americans to drink—*and comment on*—all varieties of Bigelow tea, not just Constant Comment.

THE VISION THING

To Each Bigelow Generation Its Own Vision

One of Cindi's mission statement-like quotes is that Bigelow's tea must be "innovative, nimble and focused."

To me, "nimble and focused" describes an element of vision—much like Forest & Trees Vision. She is intent on scaling volume but never at the expense of quality. She constantly explores other food products that pull that off.

In following her vision, Ruth sacrificed all she had worked for when she entered supermarkets, but she never considered sacrificing quality, which necessitated a price five times Lipton's, one of the big risk factors she faced.

Vision Chart

(For chapter 11)

▶ Sometimes, long-term vision is impractical. Adding an intermediate vision may be helpful. Ruth's vision—everyone drinking Bigelow

Tea—was supplemented by her intermediate goal and strategy—placement on supermarket shelves, next to Lipton.

▶ Ruth was willing to "go for broke" to achieve her vision. Sometimes that is necessary. Most often, it is possible to moderate the risk, for example, by staging a series of steps toward the goal.

The Vision Transition

One way Cindi pursued quality is by developing an extraordinary taste talent. She works hard at that, drinking at least 500 competitive teas a year, which she believes has brought Bigelow's devotion to quality "to a whole new level" (similar to the Terlatos' self-taught wine tasting expertise).

It took decades for Bigelow Tea to become the kind of success it now knows. Contrast Jim Covert who was thrown into the pool and with great coaches, learned to swim. Then he was thrown, over and over, into ever deeper pools, each time learning a new stroke and winning a series of medals.

CHAPTER 12

James M. Covert

James M. Covert Found Security in Serendipity

▼▼▼▼▼▼▼▼▼▼▼▼

*J*im Covert was an army brat who became a self-taught rock guitarist picking his way to record gold before being drafted and shipped to
Viet Nam. While in Asia,, he impressed someone and ultimately was
picked for the Secret Service to protect Presidents Nixon, Ford and Carter
while learning to build a more secure White House. Security systems define
his career as founder of SecurityLink here and distant firms in Australia for
one. His career unfolded serendipitously as bit by bit he applied Rapid Action
Vision that employed his many talents, including the rollup of one room mom
& pop security firms into huge, efficient firms that pleased customers with
unaccustomed but eagerly sought superior service aspects.

What Do The Doors and the Secret Service Have in Common?

Jim Covert's life story seems the epitome of serendipity. In high school, his
cousin, Lester (Cookie) Van Dyke, the father of comedians Dick and Jerry
Van Dyke, helped Jim get a job as rhythm guitarist for Chess Records. Jim

had five gold and two platinum records before he was 18. He played with the Shadows of the Night, Chubby Checkers, Chuck Berry, Lionel Richie, and Smokey Robinson. He dropped out of college to travel and play guitar with Jim Morrison and his *The Doors* co-founder, Ray Manzarek. So far, serendipity served him well. However, no longer eligible for the college student deferment, he was drafted and sent to Asia. [Covert #1]

Was his serendipity ended by that deployment? Not Quite. Actually, it freed-up Jim for the next positive outcome.

While Jim was overseas, someone had taken notice of his work, and he was recruited into the U.S. Secret Service.

It turned out that he was too young for the Secret Service—he was not yet 21, the minimum age. So they had to create a special exemption for Jim. But then, he certainly had the most appropriate surname of any covert Secret Service agent.

Finishing second in class at the Secret Service Academy, he was immediately assigned to the White House detail.

The Secret Service has many functions, not just protecting presidents, and has many offices outside Washington, D.C. It is unusual for a newly graduated agent to be assigned to the White House, let alone to the president's detail.

Over the years, Jim followed President Richard Nixon on his first trip to China, and guarded Gerald Ford and Jimmy Carter, as well as Anwar Sadat when he was with Carter during their Camp David Talks. Serendipity marches on. [Covert #2]

In those years, the Secret Service, through its Technical Service Division ("TSD"), handled all the electronic security for the White House, the Treasury building, the CIA facilities, and former presidents' houses. Along the way, Jim was selected to work with TSD in addition to his other duties. Perhaps in those days, when no one had even dreamed of cyber security, mastering the electronic guitar was a sufficient qualification for TSD.

In that capacity, he worked alongside people from ADT, a private sector security giant, and a subcontractor of TSD, where TSD monitored ADT's work installing systems according to TSD's directions.

Several years later, Jim left government and went to work for a security company in California. The owner of that company, billionaire Stewart Resnick, enabled Jim to start a new company, SecurityLink. Jim developed Trend Pattern Vision which enabled him to observe ADT as it wired government buildings under his (TSD's) "supervision."

He was said to be a veritable sponge, learning the overall business from his first employer in the field, Stewart Resnick, while devoting himself to performing his specific operational functions in flawless fashion. He observed opportunities, internal and external, and learned how to adapt them to his situation and activities.

When ADT was bought by a foreign company, the U.S. government was about to fire them: our security can not be controlled by a foreign company. Jim was new to the industry but Trend Pattern Vision was always working for him. He learned of ADT's problem. He approached the Secret Service, seeking to take over the government contract when ADT was fired.

The Secret Service countered that Jim should buy ADT's government business and the employees that served it, to assure consistency and prevent disruption of service.

Jim explained that he had neither the knowledge nor the contacts to arrange for the necessary financing.

They said "no problem" and introduced Jim to someone they knew could be of help. With a single telephone call, the financing was arranged: the go-to guy was none other than Alan Greenspan, now former Chairman of the Federal Reserve Bank.

With the government contracts as a business and credibility base, Jim was able to generate substantial non-government commercial work. Things were looking up.

Then down. A few years later. The bank that did the financing was adversely affected by the Savings & Loan crisis that paralyzed banking for years and cost the U.S. billions.

The financing bank's hands were tied. They couldn't offer a second round loan, and Jim almost lost the company. Jim had a great vision for the company. Peculiarly, that vision was inhibited by his vision of his vision. He sought help to learn how to portray his vision and his track record.

A last ditch effort worked. Jim got the financing. Not long after, the company was sold to Ameritech and Jim profited handsomely, though his share was not as large as his investors'. [Covert #3]

Bound by his non-compete contract with Ameritech, Jim left for Australia and New Zealand, where he founded similar companies that ultimately became the biggest in the industry in those two countries. There too, a lack of follow-on equity promised by the initial investor prevented Jim from profiting.

In both situations, Jim quickly assessed the business situations (Rapid Action Vision). His antennae, however, so keenly focused on markets, competition and employees, seemed far less sharp when it came to arranging financings.

About two years later, Covert returned to the U.S., where Beyond-the-Eaves and Trend Pattern Visions kicked in. He learned that Ameritech was interested in selling SecurityLink. Lesson learned. This time, he arranged the financing with GTCR, a private equity firm run by Bruce Rauner, now governor of Illinois.

In January, 2001, Jim and his partners bought SecurityLink back for a few hundred million dollars, and in July of that same year, they sold SecurityLink to ADT for over $1 billion. Jim knew he'd sell to ADT even before he bought back SecurityLink, the result of Beyond-the-Eaves and Trend Pattern Vision, and he was ready to act before others could because of Rapid Action Vision. Since then, Covert and his partners have successfully bought and sold a couple more security companies. [Covert #4]

▼▼▼▼▼▼▼▼▼▼▼▼▼▼▼▼▼▼▼▼▼▼▼▼▼▼▼▼▼▼▼▼

Is Serendipity Guided by Luck … or Pluck?

Serendipity has been defined as "the occurrence and development of events by chance in a happy or beneficial way." That would seem to be an inherent contradiction of vision. One hardly needs to be a visionary to succeed if the outcome is guided by chance. Of course, not everything is serendipitous.

Favorable outcomes may seem serendipitous when they actually are the result of skill, dedication and hard work. Wise parents tell their kids luck is what you make it and how prepared you are to take advantage of opportunities when they come along. I would add that you also must be able to spot opportunity before and more clearly than others do. That's an important add-on to vision. Still, in such circumstances, vision is often an operative factor. It helps but isn't determinative.

Some occurrences may seem anything but happy or beneficial. They may knock you for a loop and prevent your progress. At the time, development may seem like a wreck. Occasionally, the derailment prevents a worse outcome or can even constitute teeing you up for bigger and better results.

▲▲▲▲▲▲▲▲▲▲▲▲▲▲▲▲▲▲▲▲▲▲▲▲▲▲▲▲▲▲▲▲

That summary of Jim's career seems like a series of disjointed steps, each resulting in a favorable next step, generally as a result of unplanned, externally prompted occurrences. In other words, serendipity. It is difficult to conjure up how vision drove this success, when each of the next steps became available by external intervention and by chance. Yet there were indeed visions. Jim didn't have a single vision spreading over many years. He had a series of separate visions, each lasting for a short time, until the next occurred.

In the early years—military, Secret Service—Jim was following the fine example set by his father, a lieutenant colonel paratrooper in World War II, and "a real American hero," as Jim describes him. Constantly relocating from one military base to another, Jim had been in eight schools by sixth grade. His father, whom he loved, was tough and that applied to Jim too. So Jim learned quickly to gauge new situations, with what I will call Rapid Response Mechanisms (RRMs), what others have referred to as the sixth sense: rapid recognition from experience. I think it is part of Rapid Action Vision. In any event, Jim used this to make friends quickly.

His RRM enabled Jim to make friends quickly even in high school. What it really taught him was how to be dropped into a situation, to assess the terrain, and to figure out what needed to be done to achieve a short-term goal. Then he had the skills to implement. [Covert #5] RRM can be extended into vision, when it is more than reactionary and is purposeful and knowingly applied. But Rapid Action Vision may not be sufficient by itself. Jim had a combination of Rapid Action Vision, Beyond-the-Eaves Vision, and Trend Pattern Vision, the last two enabled him to see an industry and cut to its essence.

▼▼▼▼▼▼▼▼▼▼▼▼▼▼▼▼▼▼▼▼▼▼▼▼▼▼▼▼▼▼

The Missing Credential on Veteran Resumes

We hear that veterans are great candidates for business jobs. Most don't fully understand why that's true, perhaps assuming it's a platitude of gratitude for extraordinary service to country. Beyond that, what generally comes to mind—discipline, commitment, leadership, obedience—is not the whole story.

Rapid Action Vision is often a skill developed by people who have served in the military. They are trained to develop a Rapid Response Mechanism so they can be dropped into a dangerous situation and have the ability to determine the necessary response quickly. In *Invent Reinvent Thrive,* I described this skill in the story of Nir Barkat, who went from soldier to business tycoon to Mayor of Jerusalem. In the military, RRM often makes the difference between life and death. RRM can be expanded to Rapid Action Vision and be carried over and applied to the business arena, where it can prove very valuable, although not determinative of life and death.

RRM is not exclusively based on military experience. First responders tend to have RRM, and some can expand it to Rapid Action Vision in business applications. One can imagine that RRM is a survival instinct in other dangerous professions, such as substitute teachers. Athletes often have such skills, but their ability to convert it to business arenas depends on the extent to which they actually developed RRM or Rapid Action Vision or merely relied on their coach's vision.

Jim wasn't totally reliant on Rapid Action Vision to make friends; he had considerable talents in his arsenal. In high school, Jim taught himself to play guitar and joined a band: not a bad way to be popular and make friends.

Growing up on military bases and learning about life from a tough colonel father, he knew what to do and how to act in the military. That disciplined work and Rapid Action Vision, which he had developed even before entering the military, including knowing how to make friends quickly, made for a successful governmental career.

▼▼▼▼▼▼▼▼▼▼▼▼▼▼▼▼▼▼▼▼▼▼▼▼▼▼▼▼▼▼▼▼

CEOs Take Note: You can't Ad Lib Rapid Action Vision

One should not confuse Rapid Action Vision with improvisation. They are different skills. Ask the coach:

Years ago, Northwestern University football coach Gary Barnett guest-lectured in one of my classes and explained to my students that before every one of his 60-plus team practices, he spent over an hour preparing the 15-second message he'd give to his team. Extraordinary effort with equally extraordinary results: in two years, he led what had been a mediocre team to playing in the Rose Bowl game.

Then on two subsequent occasions, Barnett gave impromptu press conferences with embarrassing results.

I wondered how someone who was able to deliver such extraordinarily insightful and motivational 15-second speeches to his players could fall on his face at press conferences.

During one Academy Awards show, host Billy Crystal delivered the seemingly perfect ad lib to smooth over an inappropriate comment by an elderly honoree. I marveled at the ad lib. Crystal later indicated that his apparent ad lib line was anything but that. He rehearsed 5,000 jokes and ad lib lines beforehand, knowing he might use just a few during the show.

That's when it struck me: Coach Barnett was an expert at brief, cogent messages after he had done his one hour homework—a rate of 240 times the length of each 15-second message. That may indicate great homework skills but not ad lib talent.

The only difference between Coach Barnett and Billy Crystal: Billy knew his limitations and planned accordingly.

Of course he also had the extraordinary skill of recalling and instantly retrieving and delivering the line with a comedian's superb timing when needed. Most important, he made it seem like ad lib. That's why he gets to host the Oscars.

Know your skills and their limitations. Good, dedicated homework skills are the universal enhancer, especially for the would-be visionary.

▲▲▲▲▲▲▲▲▲▲▲▲▲▲▲▲▲▲▲▲▲▲▲▲▲▲▲▲▲▲▲▲▲▲▲▲

Ameritech had not perceived the essence of the security alarm business. Indeed, while they were able to increase revenue because of their huge customer base, they were unable to master a couple of simple points. Those points guided Jim in his management and ownership of SecurityLink, both before sale and for the six months after its re-acquisition until it was resold.

Jim explained it with an example. It seems Ameritech had increased revenue multifold over what it was when they acquired it from Jim. However, in those short couple of years, Ameritech managed to convert a handsome profit into a loss.

Jim believes that was the result of bad service and inattention to customer needs. Jim says virtually no one cancels their alarm system company, unless they are moving to a new house or facility or have failed to receive proper service. Therefore, Jim figured that the best way to eliminate attrition of the customer base was to provide that service continually.

That's simple: In addition to forms of vision, Jim had some simple tenets that guided him throughout his amazing career in that industry. Time after time, such principles enabled a recurring monthly rate and return, or the maintenance and growth of revenue and income in a business that valued continuity and regularity of performance with a handsome multiple. As a result, each of the companies in that field that Jim and his partners acquired were sold at substantial profits in relatively short periods of time.

Jim also had Trend Pattern Vision that was flawless when it came to advancements in the industry, but was less than comparable when it came to finance.

In an industry where technology was having a serious impact, it was possible to create huge value by "rolling up" a series of small mom-and-pop companies, almost all of which operated out of a single room. He'd combine them in a series of acquisitions into an efficient single operation. Then, managerial and operational efficiencies, good service and careful branding created a viable organization that could be sold to others at a price far above the sum of their original acquisition prices.

In all, Jim acquired 176 mom and pop businesses and used these basic principles to integrate them into compelling and vastly more valuable targets for big acquisitions.

THE VISION THING

Vision: The Space Between Blinks

Rapid Action Vision is not so much a different kind of vision that interacts with other elements of visions. It is much like an adjective modifying in sense of time, the other elements of vision that are like nouns. Where others might take years to respond to new terrain or circumstances, Covert often took months or even just weeks to respond to the same situations. That seemed perfectly appropriate given the span of their respective visions.

Rapid Action Vision: A Remedy For Some of Today's Rapidity

Today, everything is faster and is expected to be. Everything comes at us faster and closer. While that may make challenges and opportunities more visible, the need to adjust more quickly is more difficult. Perhaps a story will explain.

One of my grandsons, a top student and varsity baseball player failed the eye exam portion of his driver's license test. He explained that he never had a problem in class because his mother had told him to always sit in the front row. Yes, but how was he able to hit a fast ball, which he did quite well? Weeks after he started wearing contacts, I asked whether it helped his batting. "Papa," he said, "now, I can actually see the ball leave the pitcher's hand."

Covert would be the first to tell you that he hasn't always read people as well as he needed to, especially in finance, as described earlier in this chapter and in personal relations. He also says that most of his mistakes in personal relations resulted from spending too much time focused on business. Some people have a different quality of vision in different arenas such as business on the one hand and family on the other. More often the quality of vision difference is the result of limited and insufficient time, attention and focus.

Vision Chart

(For Chapter 12)

▶   When a market seems well-served, many will say "if it ain't broke, don't fix it." But the market has limited information and knowledge. Your vision to better serve the market, based on the results of your good homework, may prove valuable. People were "satisfied" with their home or store security systems, even though they had complaints. Then Jim showed them a better way.

▶   Improving your ability to quickly see opportunity when you're dropped into a new situation could prove valuable. You can create exercises for yourself, and every day, life provides opportunities to develop those skills. Life generally provides easier, less time-intensive solutions that obviate the need for Rapid Action Vision. But when opportunities calling for instant action arise, having Rapid Action Vision capabilities can prove very valuable.

▶   Visions aren't limited to a "picture" of a business as a whole. It can also be a vision of tenets or principles of business. Jim's tenets related to loyalty and basic business principles, such as good service. He repeatedly applied that general vision of how business should run to a number of different enterprises.

The Vision Transition

Jim Covert is a baby boomer. Well ahead of his time, his employment pattern resembles that of a millennial: constant rotation in and out of jobs. He has had more jobs than the average millennial will experience in a lifetime. That vocational mobility and his unique visions were how Jim developed the skill, experience and network to become a giant in his industry.

David Abney has had only one employer, UPS. He too has had several jobs but all at UPS. Like Covert, David Abney has developed considerable skills, experience and network. Those and his vision resulted in his becoming a giant in his industry.

CHAPTER 13

David Abney

A Study in Brown: UPS Can't Turn Back Time

▼▼▼▼▼▼▼▼▼▼▼

*W*hen David Abney became UPS's CEO he inherited a decision to automate drivers' routes made after their average delivery cycle was complicated by a blizzard of new elements. Result: deliveries were to be made within hours not within the old five or six days. The era brought packages from disparate clients, some arriving by air, some by rail. UPS needed vexing algorithms to puzzle out the variables. CEOs habitually drop old boss visions, especially ones that no one believes in. But Abney stayed the course, modifying the old vision hoping to make it work. But could all the team's horsepower and its engineering smarts resolve the enigma?

Brown Trucks In a Kaleidoscope World

Everyone has seen the brown UPS trucks piloted by deliverers clad in brown. That part of the company hasn't changed much in a hundred years. However, almost everything else about the company has changed.

Early on, UPS operations –all ground delivery, usually for department stores to their customers, with all deliveries being treated equally and without special timing or handling—was dominated by Frederick Taylor-like efficiencies. Delivery and pick-up routes were based on geography loops—starting in one place, following the loop of best fit, and winding up back at the starting point. Along the way, the driver made an average of 125 stops. Any college graduate was smart enough to use the best fit loop model and plot his route for the day. [Abney #1]

Customers rarely questioned delivery and pick up timing. I once asked a retailer about the then standard "6 day or so" delivery policy but was told there was no alternative. I never asked again. The stores and their customers were satisfied, so in the vein of "ignorance is bliss," the process became embedded. It fit the needs of a more leisurely yesterday.

But as time passed, the business changed—becoming a business with mixed air and ground operations, new services and delivery windows, even set delivery times, and new customer categories. It became a business with exacting needs and with substantially increased volume, making "simple" delivery routes *far more complex*. The only thing that stayed the same: 125 stops on the average driver's daily route.

Those of us who rely on an iPhone to keep us on track, aren't as demanding as UPS drivers. If a stop on our route takes two minutes longer, so be it. If, you're a UPS driver, making 125 stops, two minutes more a stop is 250 additional minutes. Your seven hour day just became 50% longer. Actually, "*far more complex*" doesn't begin to explain it.

David Abney had been one of those UPS drivers. He certainly grasped that drivers were plagued by the increased route complexity.

In 1974, two years before he graduated from Delta State University, located in Cleveland, Mississippi, where David was born, Abney went to work for UPS: not as an executive or salesman but in the warehouse. Then, sheepskin in hand, he was promoted to driver in a brown uniform in one of those boxy brown UPS vans. UPS was then a 69 year old company with approximately 17,000 employees. He clearly started at the bottom.

By 2014, 38 years after David's graduation, the company had over 400,000 employees, and David had ascended from COO, responsible for leading changes in day-to-day operations and global expansion, to CEO.

David knows, first-hand, how route complexity has increased. The number of factors affecting route planning began to exceed the drivers' mental capabilities. This was not a driver short-coming. The best MIT PhDs couldn't have handled all those factors in their heads.

David explained the extent of the new complexities: "In what we would call a simple 125-stop route in any given day, there are more decisions (by outside forces that confronted their vans) than there are milliseconds in the history of mankind."

David says UPS has the actual number: Trillions upon trillions of decisions, in fact. One can't fathom such numbers. They overwhelm. UPS hoped that computer algorithms could solve this dilemma. [Abney #2]

The program the former managers devised was known as Orion. Research on Orion began in 2003. It took five years to get the algorithm to produce acceptable results and another four years to determine how to properly use and deploy the new tool. This included testing methods and procedures, new metrics and learning how to educate the UPS people.

Small scale deployment began in 2012; full scale in 2013. By the time David became COO, development of Orion was "right in my area of responsibility, and there was total darkness at the end of the tunnel.

"Top-level management had serious doubts that they would succeed. Few believed current technology was up to the challenge." Those doubts were the immovable object to the irresistible force of David's vision of a new and better UPS and the engineering prowess of his team.

When UPS went public, a Wall Street analyst said: "One of UPS's competitors is a marketing company that happened to be in transportation. But UPS is an engineering company that happened to be in transportation." [Abney #3]

Worse yet, the drivers were convinced that the project would fail; they felt that nothing could make them more efficient, though they desperately hoped something could.

David Abney has been the CEO of UPS, since 2014, and he is not leaving anytime soon. Still, I asked him what advice he would give his successor. He said: "In your previous job, you may have been focused on what's working today and in the immediate future and realize how successful you've been.

"But [as UPS's CEO] your job is about seeing what's going to happen in the future and getting ready for [where] UPS is going to be five, ten, or more years away. So you've got to have much more forward vision." [Abney #4]

He had great confidence in UPS people—drivers and engineers. Over ten years of seemingly wasted hard work by respected, capable people. Over ten years of top management allocating valuable manpower and substantial capital sunk in a deep hole. A new CEO might well be tempted to cut the losses—readily attributable to his predecessor—and start his realm with a clean slate, unburdened by the past.

But Abney had a Forest & Trees Vision, where the forest consisted of customers' needs and the trees consisted of UPS's skill.

David saw that a UPS solution would solve customers' problems. So what did Abney do? He doubled down and pushed Orion forward.

Abney saw Orion as feeding an important, indeed a critical need. "It just seems like we didn't have much of a choice, that the complexity was getting greater and greater, so we had to find a way to do this.

"We all believed that you could do it. I don't believe that we thought it was going to take as many years as it did."

Abney also had Trend Pattern Vision. David believed that the complicating factors impacting delivery routes would only get worse and he saw trends in technology's ability to deal with big data.

THE VISION THING

David's Vision Led to an Unexpected Outcome

So, is belief the essence of vision? Remember how Ross Perot Jr. believed in his father's vision? To be a visionary, must one be a believer or have followers who are believers? Actually, belief may have driven persistence. However, the vision resulted from something else.

Instead of viewing the outcome as binary—success or failure, David urged the team to dig deeper: learn what worked and what didn't. It turns out that what wasn't working reflected inadequate mapping.

David saw that UPS's engineering expertise was being applied to a problem in the UPS way. The UPS way didn't just happen. It needed to be managed, to be coaxed and supported periodically. And it needed to be motivated and incentivized continually.

Good engineers, like many professionals, are prone to continue what they've done before, because it always worked before. It's difficult enough to elicit change when an approach doesn't work. Even then, change is difficult and often a choice of last resort. But when things have been going well, why would you change what you are doing?

At this highly disciplined company, the R&D work was being conducted by teams that included those who previously had been UPS drivers. And, as you remember, they didn't believe their routing could be improved. Interestingly, at one point, certainly when David was driving a UPS truck and likely more recently than that, they were correct, because standard "6 day or so" delivery meant dealing with fewer data points. The technology wasn't developed to the point that it could handle disparate sources of packages or, say, overnight deliveries.

Fortunately, the need for change was apparent to the drivers, and that was reinforced by another standard UPS procedure: listening.

Abney is a big believer in listening. During his first year as CEO, he visited UPS customers and employees worldwide, without preconceive notions, he listened to their needs and wants. He views listening as a building block to constructing his vision.

David trusted his team's engineering expertise. Their product reflected the fact that "they measure everything in tenths of seconds." The way I would put it: The problem was that they were intent on selling their inventory—the service or solution they already had, which happened to be good. David wanted them to focus on the customers' pain points to see trends he saw that would exacerbate current problems.

He had to work across internal disciplines, such as sales and R&D and, if necessary to expand his focus to other companies and industries.

He used Beyond-the-Eaves Vision to learn better ways to develop new solutions, new products or services, to sell to the UPS customers.

Now he had to get his team to listen to customers and the drivers. And he had to get everyone to believe. He had to teach them to expand their vision beyond their current capabilities, to focus on the goal, to do their homework, and then to use their expertise to solve the problem. [Abney #5]

David's secret solution wasn't to get UPS employees to listen to him but to get them to listen to their customers, each other and even other businesses and industries. "Some of the brightest people I've ever met…are so bright that they sometimes forget to listen. And you can learn so much more if you're willing to do that," David said to me. [Abney #6]

But the Orion project hadn't been just a failure to listen. Everybody understood that they needed to improve logistics and dispatching processes and that eventually technology would provide a solution.

"[We] had made earlier attempts to get our arms around this. We weren't able to do it, because technology wasn't developed yet to the extent we needed it," David said.

So what made David confident that it was the right time to push ahead after seven years of effort without successfully attaining the objective? It comes back to good homework. They determined that the technology had evolved enough to do the job with suitable data. The problem was they needed more data. [Abney #7]

The data, equal to many trillions of choices—truly "big-data"—was available, but first this big data had to be gathered. By this time the algorithms and computers needed to handle all this data had become available. The rest of the story was one of good engineering, all brilliantly executed. None of that would have been possible without the unique combination of visions employed by David Abney.

CEO David Abney modified an old vision, an improved form of Retro Vision. He avoided an all too common new CEO gambit of trashing the prior CEO's plans. Instead, he identified new progress patterns and trends in big data processing. He felt company advances would solve the problem. He surprised drivers and some managers by squiring the risk-laden plan to fruition and large UPS success. Thanks to his success, UPS remains an investors' darling. [Abney #8]

Vision Chart

(For Chapter 13)

▶ A vision is only as good as its feasibility and a vision can go stale because no one sees the wherewithal to achieve the goal. Then, there is a tendency to abandon the vision. It may be worth revisiting the vision, from time to time, in light of technological advancements, just as Abney did.

The Vision Transition

Most people consider UPS and FedEx two peas in a pod, competing in a lost world where Currier and Ives maps prevail. But today's world is where couriers drive trucks and companies. In reality, David Abney and UPS are quite different than Fred Smith and Federal Express.

That I was fortunate to interview both for this book is happenstance. That the chapters about them abut is more to demonstrate the differences. The leaders are both smart, but one is a founder and has run the company for decades; the other started in the warehouse when the company was well established. One drove trucks for the company the other flew planes before he set up FedEx. One firm first dictated terms to customers, then developed a system to comply with customers' demands. The other gambled big on giving information to the customer, a company, not customer, initiating change.

CHAPTER 14

Fred Smith

Smith's 'Flights of Fancy' Still Bring Fancy Profits

▼▼▼▼▼▼▼▼▼▼▼▼▼

*F*red Smith's remarkable vision did not end when he proved overnight air delivery of package mail at an elevated price was doable at high profit. What made Smith a stand out in a short list of top visionaries was a world view that equipped him to find lucrative new ways to leapfrog dated commercial methods. His outlook reflects broad study of social, demographic, technological, geographic and business trends. He combines this knowledge with a traditional mentality, even humility that belies his reputation. He nurtures and listens to inside talent and seeks outside expertise to solve problems such as computer security he knows he cannot expect to understand. Smith's decision to let customers track packages real time reflects but one of Fred's key visions. Those enable Smith to continue growing FedEx in an unrivaled reign over a great company that approaches half a century.*

When the Fastest Distance Between Two Points Is Not a Straight Line

If you were in Los Angeles and you wanted to go to San Francisco would you fly to Memphis first? If you were a package, young Fred Smith felt you should fly to Memphis first whether you were in Los Angeles, Miami or Seattle: indeed any place in America.

That's because a universal hub made sense even if his Yale professor gave him a C on a paper outlining such a remote home base in his preposterous Memphis-first delivery plan.

After all, nobody else had tried such a cockamamie idea. Perhaps the professor thought the gregarious young man before him, a notable Yale party person, was whacked. But the plan was meticulously drawn—too precise for a 'C' Fred thought.

Fred himself set the idea aside when he graduated from Yale. Hardly cowed by the professor's view of him, Fred applied himself and graduated with honors. He might have attempted to commercialize the Yale class concept, but such thoughts had to be deferred. Fred joined the United States Marines and was promptly sent to the war in Viet Nam.

Fred learned to fly at age 15 and became a crop dusting star back home in Mississippi: The Marine Corps was delighted to have him. He flew 200 ground support combat missions as a Captain. He earned the Silver Star and a bronze medal. He got a pair of purple hearts during two tours of serious combat. Fred was clearly a war hero but isn't one to accept that designation.

Fed up with the violence of war at his discharge, he was quoted in Current Biography Yearbook (2000) saying that he "got so sick of destruction and blowing things up…that I came back determined to do something more constructive."

Most people credit Fred Smith with being a great visionary because he founded Federal Express. He was. But most people misunderstand his initial vision. He did start Fed Ex to compete with the U.S. Post Office but not to carry letters and documents.

In fact, federal laws—the private express laws dating back to 1792—barred Postal rivals until eight years after Federal Express had started. Besides, that business dropped off a cliff when fax machines became prevalent. Then it nearly died as emails and scanned documents became ubiquitous.

Smith started FedEx to move high-tech products, such as computer components. They were too valuable to trust to the USPO in those days. What Smith envisioned, in addition to providing comfort of timely delivery of high-value/low weight products, was a means by which users could control inventory costs, by moving items to customers' balance sheets rapidly.

That was in 1971. So much has changed since and much of the change affected FedEx. Remarkably, Smith has continued throughout to be a serial visionary and a successful one at that.

Essentially, Smith divides the job of a CEO of any big business into two separate but related parts. The first part is leadership: selecting the best high-level executives, while creating and being part of a collaborative group that develops strategies and guides their effective implementation. The second part is being a visionary: "having a view of the future and understanding where the organization has got to go to be successful within those future parameters," as he put it. [Smith #1]

That self-inclusive definition may sound like a given when one is analyzing a true visionary. One might easily be tempted to attribute that capability to some inborn, natural powers: that a true visionary is born with special powers that reveal the future. Attributing Smith's powers of vision to a special gift is an over-simplified approach to understanding visionaries.

Another way is to attribute it to luck: the lucky guy just happened upon the idea. After all, Fred Smith is often perceived as the quintessential example of entrepreneurial luck. The story is legion: FedEx was hanging on by a thread, as do many startups. But FedEx was different.

Founded in 1971, Federal Express was two years old when the Arab Embargo began, elevating the price of oil several fold and thus of airplane fuel to a point where FedEx's breakeven point was pushed out by at least two years.

Fred had been great at raising equity investment from traditional sources: venture capital firms, including First Chicago Investment Corp. and Heizer Corp. The embargo brought an abrupt halt to the flow of VC money. Fred was squeaking by. Inevitably he was faced with the business-man's nightmare: a looming shortfall and insufficient funds to pay it.

So Fred went to Las Vegas and gambled a precious $5,000. He went to the blackjack tables and bet his cards carefully. Luck was with him; he won $24,000, enough to cover towering fuel bills.

His Federal Express was able to hang on as trade grew. So attributing his vision to luck wouldn't seem out of line. But doing so is simply all wrong. [Smith #2]

Fred certainly has some natural gifts: high intellect being one. However, each of his important visions at FedEx was the result of specific processes he had developed and uses with extraordinary dedication, discipline and skill. I dare say that those processes are near scientific and therefore are replicable.

However Fred came upon his original vision for FedEx, whether by special powers, scientific method or otherwise, he didn't rely on such means alone: He explained this process; "We had not one, not two, but three separate independent studies that showed the need for the service we were going to provide. The evidence was overwhelming that our innovative service would be better than what people could get at that time.

Fred Smith believed that "As long as we could market the service effectively, people would buy it."

Fred's primary focus was not FedEx's future. He focused first on the future of the world and then thought about the implications of that future world to FedEx. "Business success comes from effectively looking at societal change, whether it's demographic change or geopolitical expecta-tions. [Smith #3]

"Management must develop strategies that position Fed Ex to benefit when that future arrives," he said.

Fred is a prodigious reader of nonfiction books. He is especially fond of history and economics. He derives many of his visions of where the world is heading through his reading.

His selection of books is anything but random. He follows the recom-mendations of folks at the Sunday New York Times, The Harvard Business Review, and The Council on Foreign Relations. He chooses books that will help him understand and gain insight into things occurring globally and domestically that he can apply to FedEx. I find this an intellectual, even scholarly approach. I like to think it echoes Beyond-the-Eaves Vision and Trending Pattern Vision, two of the key vision elements I have designated for this book. [Smith #4]

Fred believes "If you're running a company like ours, you've got to have a significant interest in all sociological issues. I think we try to stay at least one or two generations in advance of what I think the competition is going to be doing. Sometimes we go down a rabbit hole that doesn't work. But we're trying to stay out there a couple of generations ahead."

Clearly this is a serial process for Fred: "Because all innovations tend to be commoditized pretty quickly. And so you have to be going on to the next thing. That's why I said, 'the whole process at FedEx is to try to look at the macro environment, the sociological issues, the demographics, the geo-political landscape,' and say, 'alright, this is where people are going to have a changed need, and what can we do to do that better for them?'" [Smith #5]

Fred Smith tries "To see a lot of things and read a lot of things which aren't necessarily just on FedEx, but around the environment that we are living in. A good example of that would be an effort on my part to really understand what mobility means: this proliferation of smart phones and so forth. So we've been very active getting our apps out there and trying to see.

"We work at understanding whether Apple Pay is going to be the way people pay in the future, as opposed to credit cards or debit cards. Things like the urbanization in certain parts of the world: should we have a facility here or have a facility there or make a bigger bet on Argentina or not make a bet on Argentina, whatever the case may be."

Beyond-the-Eaves Vision Does Not Exist in a Void

Fred Smith's reading of books is but one of several techniques for developing Beyond-the-Eaves Vision. In a country that published over 300,000 new and re-edition titles in 2015, it is difficult to know which of the thousands of titles to read. Fred resorted to published lists and recommendations, in the New York Times and Harvard Business Review. Many business people seek referral advice from mentors, colleagues and friends.

Larry Levy, founder of Levy Restaurants, whom I interviewed and wrote about in *Invent Reinvent Thrive*, prefers magazines and reads many different ones each month. He feels magazines give him a sense of consumer tastes and preferences. This, has been Levy's target, as food provider to millions of consumers yearly at sports venues, restaurants, and theme parks.

More recently, Levy reviews his magazines electronically. The method of receiving media is irrelevant. The key is to develop Beyond-the-Eaves Vision through an intellectual curiosity that seeks to understand what others are doing that can be adopted for direct value to the visionary.

Reading is but one route to discovery. Inventors are often inspired by nature. But we are not discussing invention here; we are referring to copying ways of advancing and improving business operations. Even that is not limited to reading for inspiration. In a world of 24/7 news coverage, YouTube, and expanded ability to travel and see new things, the world is indeed the oyster of business visionaries.

Smith also listens to his team, paying close attention to the sub-messages of people he respects like Jim Barksdale. His continued conversations with Jim after he left the company resulted in FedEx becoming an early Internet participant.

"Jim Barksdale had been our COO. We talked every week; he was a member of the strategic management committee. "He was telling me about this development at the University of Illinois—Mosaic (a pioneer internet browser that is credited with moving the World Wide Web to center stage).

"So, Barksdale, wound up going to McCaw Cellular, a company that had been bought by AT&T. And Barksdale was subsequently in large part responsible for the cellular telephone revolution.

"Jim called asking for a meeting which he said was very important. He said, 'I'm on the horns of a dilemma, because AT&T wants me to go with them, and I think if I do, I've got a pretty good shot at being the CEO of AT&T, one of America's iconic industrial companies.'" Barksdale was a former IBMer.

"Jim went on to say, 'But I've got this guy, Jim Clark, who has this company called Netscape. And he wants me to come on board and be the CEO of it.' So my advice to Jim was, 'Golly, you made lots of money at FedEx, you made lots of money at McCaw. If I were you, based on what I just heard about this, I would take a flyer on [Netscape].'

"See, I wasn't a subject expert, I wouldn't have known what the devil Mosaic was, and who [the co-inventor of Mosaic] Mark Andreesen was. And so, hearing that, my advice to Jim was, 'you should take the Netscape offer.' And he did. We at FedEx immediately acted on that [Barksdale decision]. In fact at the first board meeting that FedEx had after Jim had taken over as CEO of Netscape, I had him come talk to our Board of Directors. As a result, we were basically the first industrial application on the Internet." [Smith #6]

A Visionary's Board Must See the Vision

I wondered how Fred was able to lead his board of directors into a vision based on technological advancements, when Fred wasn't a subject matter expert and the proposal relied solely on what he'd heard from a tech world guy. Even though Fred was sold on the net by Jim, how did he convince board members that aren't as up on the subject matter as Jim might be?

Part of the answer: the Fed Ex board was familiar with Barksdale who had been Fed Ex's COO. But that alone didn't seem sufficient.

Smith also knows what he doesn't know and stocks his company with people who are knowledgeable in areas in which he is deficient. Think of Fred as a visionary who is far-sighted, challenged in certain specific areas but who obtains 'corrective lenses' as it were—executives and directors—that clear his Beyond-the-Eaves Vision.

Fred's answer is telling: "Years and years ago, we put in place an information and technology oversight committee at the board level. That's because I believed that the technological landscape was volatile and was going to shift. We had to recruit people for our Board of Directors who were literate in that area. We did that at least 25 years ago. So it's remarked upon fairly often, now, that we're one of the few companies that had this and still has it.

"So we had people on our board like Judith Estrin, who is a genius in this area and an entrepreneur as well. And her parents were noted scientists in the IT world. Professors too. So it wasn't like speaking to a bunch of guys who didn't know a thing about IT. There was a strong cadre of people on the Board of Directors who understood the profundity of what Jim was talking about. When you asked about how I look ahead, I think we realized a long time before other people did that cyber security was going to be an enormous factor. [Smith #7]

"Maybe that was because we were big in China and the Chinese were actively involved in that area. And maybe it was because the system we operate can be used for bad things, so we were on top of it. We were way ahead of most people at putting a very big emphasis on cyber security.

"The only thing I'm amazed about is that it hadn't been mandated, particularly in the world of cyber security. We just recruited a board member who is a cyber-security expert.

"Recently, we recruited two directors at the board level, one of whom is in the midst of the Silicon Valley and the social media wars. The other one has been in the middle of cyber security issues at the National Security Agency. So it's not by accident that we have those information age capabilities.

"Rob Carter is the CIO [of Fed Ex], but in essence he's the CEO of IT, because I'm not going to sit there and argue with Rob about whether we shouldn't do this or shouldn't do that, because he has a level of expertise that's far beyond mine.

A Positive Attitude About Negative Results

"We try to do a scan of what our businesses, what are competencies are, and then say, 'these are the external factors that are going to affect this business: demographics, macroeconomics, geopolitical, technology, supply chains, mobility, e-commerce, things of that nature.'

"A good example of making a wrong call on the future would be the attempt to understand the demographics of Latin America and the roll that Miami plays in that, or the evolution of Mexico after NAFTA, and after the changes that have taken place in the last decade or so in China and what that means.

"And so it wouldn't surprise you that we bought a very good company in Mexico, several years before people really recognized that Mexico was likely to become the foundry of America, replacing a great deal of what China had done in the previous 15 years." [Smith #8]

▼▼▼▼▼▼▼▼▼▼▼▼▼▼▼▼▼▼▼▼▼▼▼▼▼▼▼▼▼▼▼

When a Visionary Needs a Visionary

It's interesting that Smith's vision of Mexico becoming America's foundry reflects the same thing Ross Perot feared (that giant sucking sound). Smith and Perot were friends. Early on, when the original Fed Ex investors were hesitant to re-up and about the time that Smith took his desperate trip to Las Vegas to win the payroll, Smith offered Perot the opportunity to buy 34% of FedEx. Perot's agreement to make that commitment motivated existing inventors to reinvest, so Perot never got to.

▲▲▲▲▲▲▲▲▲▲▲▲▲▲▲▲▲▲▲▲▲▲▲▲▲▲▲▲▲▲▲

"At one point FedEx was giving desktop computers to customers so that they could use our system to manage their inventories. That was our attempt to help customers resolve the logistics. FedEx was close to being the number one purchaser of PCs in the nation. We were putting them in shipping locations everywhere. When the Internet came about, you could get this information using any type of computer, a profound change in our favor. We were ready for this: One of the first significant industrial applications on the Internet was the ability to track packages that FedEx was moving through the system. [Smith #9]

The Perfect Gift: Trojan Horse Computers

That is not terribly unlike the technique used by American Hospital Supply Company, years ago, long before the Internet. They bought the biggest, clunkiest desktop units they could find to supply to their customers. They were single-purpose computers, directly wired to American Hospital's offices, enabling the customers to order direct but only from American Hospital on the computer. And of course people didn't want two clunky desktops on their desks, so they tended to get rid of their other computers, keeping only the one provided by American Hospital Supply. That effectively shut out American Hospital's competition.

Smith also works hard at hiring the right people. "I think the main thing is, at the top level, we have people who are really interested in doing something different and changing the world and seeing how they can modify things, who are turned on by that. I think, hopefully, I'm the band conductor, but we've got people that play the individual instruments and are willing to play jazz today and Beethoven tomorrow.

"Our CFO is a constant change agent, in terms of the way we've done our pensions, our benefits and in terms of the way we handle certain reporting requirements and the organization of the financial structure. He's constantly managing the technological seismic movements due to the digital revolution and now the Internet of Things. So I just think it's so inbred in the top management of the company that it doesn't have to be forced anymore."

Fred has been quoted as saying that he fights naysayers at FedEx but needs charisma and lobbyists (presumably both in Washington, D.C. and states) to do so. "We do get naysayers: we try to convert them. And occasionally, we just have to run over them. And even more occasionally they have to go.

"But in most cases I think we're capable of documenting the rationale to an extent that even naysayers on the front end, after a while, say 'you know, this is pretty persuasive. We do need to go in this direction.' There are times when I think I've got the facts on my side, but there are also times when they convert me.

"I'm not so stupid as to think that I'm always going to be right. I'm not going to be right on every one of them, but I do push the envelope and make people defend their positions. And if it doesn't turn out, you've got an escape route, without destroying the company."

Smith's use of reasoning, discussion and collaboration seems to be more important to him than the use of charisma or lobbyists. Another element that helps people join together to change things, as expressed by Fred Smith: "Well, a lot of times change is simple, if you realize the alternative is extinction."

A Visionary's Novel Vision of Risk

Fred is remembered for his Las Vegas financing maneuver, but he seems to be much more a risk manager than a risk taker.

"I think a lot of businesses, particularly in the financial sector, are bets, but not in an industrial setting like ours, for many reasons, not the least of which is that the assets are long-lived. You can change things but not by shorting today and going long tomorrow, so these things are educated risks.

"To use a military analogy, you don't want to risk your whole army. You have to engage in some level of risk, but you want to risk a platoon rather than the battalion and the battalion rather than the division. So you figure out ways to do what you're trying to do without completely putting in jeopardy the whole enterprise. When you see things are changing, you've got to be willing to change your strategy. We have had that happen several times, most notably after 2008, when the world changed.

"You make those decisions in our business by trying to keep both an offensive and a defensive strategy and by keeping the decisions as flexible as possible."

Fred said, "You've got to be willing to change your strategy." His other comments and behavior indicate a willingness to revise visions too, because he understands the need to reinvent his business periodically.

When I asked Fred about the speed of change, which of course is phenomenal in technology, he said, "Technology is not the heart of the business. It's the capillaries, if you will. So you can cut your finger and survive, even if it's a fairly deep cut.

"But if you get stabbed in the heart, it's fatal. That's what IBM's problem is. The heart of their business is the digital revolution and where that's taking us as businesses.

"In our business, the digital revolution is having a profound effect. So you just have to make sure that the direction that you're going is not inflexible and ill advised."

▼▼▼▼▼▼▼▼▼▼▼▼▼▼▼▼▼▼▼▼▼▼▼▼▼▼▼▼▼▼▼▼▼▼▼

Identify Your Analogy and Your Skills

Note Fred's use of military analogies. Fred's early years were largely formed by years in the U.S. military. A true hero during the Viet Nam War, it became part of his being. Your background is likely different than Fred's. You know what it is and you should try using your background as your frame of reference. That makes the terrain beyond the eaves less foreign, a goal worthy of your effort.

Few of you will combine Fred's natural gifts, his intellect, his risk management and length of service as CEO of the same company. Not everyone will glean wisdom or vision from reading, whether from books like Smith, or magazines like Levy, or the wealth of knowledge on the Web. Your technique may be totally unlike Fred's. The key is to develop a thoughtful approach that works for you. As Shakespeare said, "To thine own self be true." That can be transformative. That can convert your visions to a wealth of vision.

▲▲▲▲▲▲▲▲▲▲▲▲▲▲▲▲▲▲▲▲▲▲▲▲▲▲▲▲▲▲▲▲▲▲▲

"We celebrate and recognize people who have effected change. We're tolerant of things that don't go quite according to plan, but end up being great successes. And the things that don't work, we cut them off, and no harm, no fault. We move on to the next thing. And if something doesn't turn out, you've got an escape route you can do without destroying the enterprise."

The Amazon Paradox

FedEx has a paradoxical relationship with Amazon, a company that's both customer and competitor. Beyond-the-Eaves Vision keeps Fred thinking as if wearing Jeff Bezos' shoes, but never removing his own Fed Ex shoes.

"The reason e-commerce exists for moving lightweight things to people's residences is because we have a Postal Service. And the Postal Service makes 150 million stops each day. And they don't make 150 million stops to deliver packages.

"They make those daily stops to deliver mail. But first class in particular and other types of mail, are declining worldwide at a rate between 3% and 6% compounded annually. "So the Postal Service saw the e-commerce revolution as an opportunity where they could deliver relatively lightweight items to residences.

"And I think in Amazon's case, 85 percent of their shipments are less than five pounds. So as mail deliveries drop, cost per stop goes up. It's not clear exactly how this thing is going to work out. So, when we do our scenario planning, we try to look at different landscapes and be capable of succeeding regardless of what happens."

To some that will seem wasteful or worse: Double Vision or distracting. In fact, seeing the world's issues as binary, all black or white, is a ticket to doom. Creating multiple scenarios is more difficult and less comfortable. It is also an admission of lacking a crystal ball but ironically enables better "just-in-time" vision when all is said and done. In a way, it's a substitute for or even a component of Rapid Action Vision, enabling a business leader to react readily when others can't.

Tracking and Tracing: The FedEx Ultimate Innovation

Today, we all take for granted the ability to track, in real time, the package we ship through FedEx. It is comforting to see that your package is progressing according to plan. These are times of 'immediate gratification' and 'I want it now,' the FedEx transparency meme definitely fills a need.

It was visionary for Smith to recognize people would want the ability to track. After all, from the Pony Express through the hundreds of years of the USPO and through decades of FedEx, no one had that ability. Nor were FedEx customers demanding this, or for that matter even thinking of, such a power. Most visualized such transparency as inviting customer dissatisfaction as expectations went unmet. That view clearly was at loggerheads with Fred's.

Trend Pattern Vision and Beyond-the-Eaves Vision told Fred that such powers were enjoyed in other industries and that current technology made it feasible. Forest & Trees Vision told him that FedEx wasn't in the business of delivering packages; it was in the business of making customers comfortable enough with FedEx to hand them their packages and make them willing to pay a premium over United States Post Office prices.

As if his being prescient wasn't sufficient, Smith also undertook a great risk by offering customers such transparency.

For pleased as customers might be to track their packages, what would their reaction be if they were to witness—real time—their package going elsewhere than its intended destination?

Fred's vision told him that FedEx was good enough to make those occurrences rare, that having the customers' eyes would help correct errors quickly, and that customers would forgive such rare occurrences in return for the transparency. [Smith #10]

"I don't think any of our commercial customers said, 'Yeah. You need to give me a PC so I can track and trace.' But once they got the PC they realized that what they could do was take out 25 percent of their inventory earlier. And unfortunately, once that happened, we realized pretty quickly that people wanted a broader product line of shipping than we offered, because they didn't need everything express.

"If it was a low value item, they were just as happy if it got there in five days, as long it was delivered on the right day. Band-Aids versus defibrillators.

"So we bought a company called RPS, and developed this huge ground parcel business, which is taking market share now for 60 consecutive quarters. But again, it was doing something that the customers wanted, recognizing that and changing their behavior, because it's a constant, iterative loop. That's why change is so essential, because a consequence of something happening over here is generally that you have to react to the changed circumstances, sometimes change which you created."

THE VISION THING
An Easy-to-Read Visionary

Many of the most accomplished, successful people in many areas of expertise are unable to explain how they accomplished what led to their success. As a result, their accomplishments are attributed to their genes.

What Fred Smith provided, in addition to his extraordinary vision, is a keen understanding of his purposeful techniques and efforts to enable and facilitate his visionary skills. He explained how he chooses what to read, what he seeks from his reading—a grasp of the myriad social, demographic, economic, geopolitical, technological, and business trends—happening throughout the world and in numerous specific locales around the world.

He talked about how he then goes from those global concepts to the application developing opportunities for FedEx.

There have been innumerable studies regarding the term lengths of CEOs. The statistics are interesting. For publicly held U.S. companies, the average duration of CEO service is about 4 years, which is about the average duration of an NFL linebacker. (Concussions aren't the only cause of termination of service.)

Family businesses have much longer terms of CEO service, approximating more than a decade on average. Fred Smith has been CEO of FedEx for several decades as of this writing. That approaches a record. Fred's vision, his consistent processes including his study of what's happening and the effect this has on the company business along with his long-term perspective create many valuable lessons for other would be visionaries.

Vision Chart

(For Chapter 14)

▶ Great visionaries understand that visions don't breed in vacuums. Smith gathered eggs of knowledge in books, then fertilized them to become FedEx visions. Whether via books or other media, learn what's going on in the world. It will help you develop visions.

▶ Knowing the essence of the business you envision is critical to having a viable vision. Fred knew his vision wasn't to ship packages but to make customers trust him with their packages. You must step back from the daily grind to gain necessary perspective.

The Vision Transition

Fred Smith has enjoyed a lengthy term of service, during which he has revised his vision for FedEx many times and he continues to do so in remarkable ways. Changing visions is complex and generally difficult. For

Smith, doing so has been easier than it may seem. In that he was changing his own vision; he had no need to deal with the memory of or reverence for a predecessors' often indelible, imprints on the company. Second, Smith's considerable intellect and persistent search in books for clues as to future trends enabled him to develop visions that offered hints toward possible future developments.

IBM presents its current leadership with a very different situation. Predecessors going back to and including Tom Watson, include some superb individuals whose visions seem embedded in IBM's DNA. As evidence of that, IBM didn't give its trademark robot an "R2D3" (the next generation of R2D2) code name. It is called "Watson."

CHAPTER 15

Ken Keverian

The Visionary's Role in the
World of Tomorrow

▼▼▼▼▼▼▼▼▼▼▼▼▼

*B*ig Blue has spawned many visionaries over its century-long existence starting with Thomas J. Watson who set the tone for a company serving eager customers, the superb IBM sales 'family' and
its splendidly-enriched stockholders. During Watson's 42 years he created an
alleged monopoly in tabulating equipment leasing. And he steered Big Blue
through a Federal challenge with a visionary settlement that left the company
changed but unbowed as it moved to dominate in floor-sized main frame
computers under his son, Thomas Jr.'s leadership. IBM experienced missteps
along the way but remains world class in big data and analytics. Now under
IBM's CEO, Ginni Rometty, strategist Ken Keverian is to help guide IBM into
the Big Blue yonder and realize an improbable dream: create cognitive systems that will sustain growth in the world's standard of living. A revolution as
big as the industrial revolution, Ken says calmly. In fact, IBM is so huge and
so motivated, Big Blue can serve as a model and a building block for many
visionaries in what I call its Revolution-Devolution. That is, IBM creates new
thrusts as it dismantles yesteryear's once-visionary enterprises.

Visionaries Are Not Ninety-Seven Pound Weaklings

The 1940's back-of-the-comic-books featured an ad for Charles Atlas, the late fitness guru. The ad was about a "97 pound weakling" belittled in front of his girlfriend: in the ad a bully kicks sand in his face. Solution? Atlas's exercise regimen. Point well taken? The Atlas ad was still running in 2015 under a successor's sway. (Charles Atlas was 80 years old when he died on the day before Christmas in 1972.)

A similar prescription fits would-be business visionaries. Whatever your visionary aptitude, you can improve it. All you need is the knowledge of what to do and the will to do it.

Throughout this chapter, you'll find a few exercises I suggest. I wish I could tell you that mine are the only exercises that work. Truth is, the exercises are just common sense. So, I also urge you to develop your own additional exercises. I will show you how to do this. Unlike physical exercises, your self-developed vision exercises won't result in pulled muscles or a torn rotator cuff. In other works, you have everything to gain and nothing to lose.

This High Tide Will Not Float All Boats Equally

In the 1960's, every Sunday night, TV variety show host Ed Sullivan opened his show with: "Tonight, we have a *really* big show," and entertainer Jimmy Durante frequently interrupted audience applause with "You ain't seen nuthin' yet."

To analyze how visionaries are looking to the future, I'd like to adapt and combine those two sayings:

Tomorrow, there will be a really, *really* big show,

and You soitenly ain't seen nutin' yet.

Many business leaders are adjusting their visionary compasses, each using some or all of the vision elements I described, as well as some others. One company attempting to be at the crux of tomorrow's tomorrow is IBM. That is an audacious goal, even for a company known as "Big Blue," but IBM hasn't been called "Big Blue" for "nuttin."

Visions come in all sizes and at all stages of a company's development. This book has described founders' visions—some visions conceived before the business was launched, others spawned decades after the business was under way. This book also tells of visionaries who led firms over a hundred years old. None of those companies is more complex when it comes to vision than IBM.

Big Blue was formed in 1911. It would be hard to find so large a company with as many visions over the last 100 years. Today's CEO, Ginni Rometty, is a visionary with a grandiose plan: easily IBM's most challenging vision to date.

Your vision won't be as large as hers nor your company as big as IBM. Still, there are lessons for you in the bold plans of IBM. If IBM succeeds, it's possible for its accomplishments to trickle down, as did some of IBM's earlier successes, to benefit some smaller businesses. Some smaller businesses may be swamped by IBM's tsunami-like wave, regardless of whether the ebb or the flow. Other smaller businesses may benefit. So it pays to understand IBM's vision, to keep track of its progress and to adapt accordingly.

The Big Thing D'Jour

IBM needs to be the leader in big data if it is to maintain its preeminence. There is little doubt that Big Blue has immense capacity to churn big data, but that is only a first step.

Certainly, IBM isn't the only company whose visionary's telescope is focused on a future involving big data. You've read how David Abney's UPS business dealt with trillions and trillions of data points. And other companies, such as Google, Amazon, Uber, and Microsoft, are also dealing with big data. Some hire economists who have knowledge of both: behavioral economics and the use of big data computers, an easy example of combining multiple disciplines. Of course, those companies also hire non-economists who are computer experts in big data.

Most business visionaries in this arena have recognized that big data is just a tool; more than a tool will be needed to succeed. (In previous generations, you might have hired someone who was a mechanic to service your car. But imagine how much better you could have done had you hired a mechanic who also was a combustion engineer.)

Today, the "more" is found in the applications of the data. As such, "big data" is at best half the relevant concept. One of IBM's focuses is converting big data to extraordinary knowledge, artificial intelligence (AI), as demonstrated by its know-it-all robot affectionately and respectfully named Watson, after IBM's legendary visionary leader, the first Tom Watson, its founder.

Despite its cutesy character, Watson's AI is being applied to extremely serious problems in healthcare, industry, defense, space travel, etc. Decades ago, IBM's punch card computers churned out what was then considered large data. In this age of XXX-Large T-shirts, who would have guessed that big is bigger than large.

The size of the data is important, but most meaningful are the moves from data to information, to knowledge and now to intelligence. To learn more about IBM's goals and its leaders' visions, I had a phone conversation, meetings and a personal interview with Ken Keverian, IBM's Senior VP of Corporate Strategy. I asked Keverian whether wisdom would be Watson's next attribute. His only response: a smile.

I suggest that the "more" is also a combination of disciplines: Kay Koplovitz didn't need to bring in an outsider with "the other" discipline. Her unique position as expert in both television and geosynchronous orbiting satellites gave her a leg up.

Areas where we've seen a great deal of activity and many examples of combining disciplines are where one of the areas involves the computer or the internet.

Of course, not everyone has two disciplines. It may be necessary to hire one or two people, each with one of the desired disciplines:

We saw Fred Smith, an expert in logistics, flying and more but not in computers or IT. He became an early adopter. He hired top IT talent and brought on board members whose computer/internet expertise helped him successfully lead Fed Ex.

David Abney's ability to combine an understanding of the growing power of the computer, specifically the ability to deal with big data, with his deep understanding of UPS's logistics business made Orion feasible.

Bob Walter, an expert in distribution, saw huge opportunities but recognized their considerable attendant risks. To reduce the risks he needed another discipline, algorithmic science. So he hired Doug Linton from Carnegie Mellon, and the combined disciplines proved successful.

Multiple people to garner multiple disciplines is fine. But then you must figure out how to help them communicate with each other, how to understand each other's discipline, and how to collaborate, even if not becoming an expert in that area.

Sometimes, one of the two people is the leader of the organization. Other times the leader merely orchestrates the combination of others. Of course, the greatest orchestra leaders can play all the instruments. Similarly, the more you know about each discipline the better your chances of success.

Warning! Previously, having two disciplines or being able to attract someone with one of the two disciplines gave one a leg up. In the future, two disciplines will be mandatory for success and, in many cases, for survival.

Big Blue's Big Revolution-Devolution Vision

In the early years of the computer, IBM was able to build a computer that could handle a certain amount of data, and customers adapted their needs to what their newly acquired computer could do for them. Today, IBM is building ever more robust computers, but IBM works with customers in various industries to develop those computers and systems that can handle the algorithms and data churns needed by those companies. IBM management uses Forest & Trees Vision to understand their current capacity and what capacity they must develop but also what disciplines it doesn't need that can be unloaded. It bases many of these decisions on what it learns about the market and competition through its Beyond-the-Eaves Vision.

IBM's vision is both audacious and crucial to its future. For various reasons, IBM lagged behind others in some fundamental changes in the tech world. IBM hadn't kept up with fast-moving trends in mobile and security. In the past couple of years, through acquisitions of smaller companies, it remained relevant. It has returned to and has achieved a position of leadership in those areas and is in position to take advantage of its size, talent and reputation in inclusive areas with its big data and artificial intelligence capabilities among other special skills.

When I mentioned to Ken Keverian that IBM CEO Rometty referred to him as her choice as IBM's strategist for "the first part of IBM's transformation," Keverian humbly tried explaining that away.

That's when I questioned Ken as to why he left his job as a top managing partner at Boston Consulting Group, an eminent consulting firm that has advised more than two thirds of the Fortune 500 companies. I should add that BCG was ranked second in Fortune's 100 *Best Companies to Work For in 2015.*

'In response, he could have talked about the stature, power or compensation that came with his new position as IBM's top corporate strategist. Instead he asked me a question of his own: "How many 100+ year old computer companies can you name?"

Clearly he wanted to be engrossed in a corporate vision so all-encompassing only a giant company with the history and the resources of an IBM could pull it off. But he didn't elaborate.

What Ken *was* willing to reveal answered my question. What he said is key to understanding the stories and lessons of the successful business visionaries I interviewed for this book.

One of the things that clearly attracted Ken is the raison d'etre for Rometty's vision at IBM. She hopes to foster "future cognitive systems" that will underlie sustained growth in "the world's standard of living." In a sense, Rometty's vision both collides and blends with virtually every meaningful business vision in the world. Interestingly, Ken refers to that goal as "a revolution of the magnitude of the Industrial Revolution."

Imagine having to envision- let alone to create- a new IBM thrust, on the scale of the Industrial Revolution to provide the means of improving the *whole world's* standard of living.

Is this pie in the sky? Hardly. The computer has already revolutionized the world several times over. It has enabled many things we take for granted, things our great grandparents never could have imagined. To expand on that statement: My parents didn't ride in a car until well into their teen years, but lived to see Neil Armstrong land on the moon and shuttles fly "where no man had gone before." By the end of their lives, their watches contained more computer power than the early space ships. And that's before the Apple Watch. Only God (or Watson) knows what my great grandchildren will wear on their wrists.

As we all know, the personal computer gave immense power to the average person in recent decades. I refer to that as the greatest bloodless revolution in history.

Yet the challenge is not just starting a revolution. IBM, after all, is the antithesis of a start-up. Rometty's challenge entails simultaneously reducing IBM's current businesses, which are anything but insubstantial, while starting or acquiring new ones.

Implementing Rometty's two activities in series—ending the old businesses before beginning the new businesses—is impossible. The two drives must be made in tandem, reducing and eliminating parts of the old while infusing vitality into the new: What Ken refers to as a revolution might best be denominated a revolution-devolution.

I submit that some of the business visionaries portrayed in this book have also overseen revolution-devolutions though on a smaller scale:

- Bob Walter built Cardinal Health as he eliminated Cardinal Foods.

- Marc Schulman shuttered *Eli's: The Place for Steak* as he created the dessert colossus *Eli's Cheesecake*.

- Ross Perot disposed of his computer companies as he increased real estate and energy business holdings.

- The Bigelows eliminated gift shops as outlets as they started marketing their teas to supermarkets.

- Jim Stephen developed gas grills as he watched the inevitable market decline for Weber's iconic charcoal kettle grill.

- Bill Terlato's integration of vertical wine components including vineyards was supported while changing the focus of its wholesale bottled wine distribution business.

- Keith Williams added new businesses at UL while ridding the firm of cash draining operations and culture.

What I refer to as revolution-devolution isn't always part of a vision. Sometimes it is part of implementing the vision. The implementation is no less important than conceiving the vision: it is simply different.

Ken also provided valuable insight into my concept of Retro Vision and the basis upon which many visions depend:

Ken Keverian's comments tell me he is a firm believer in what I refer to as Retro Vision. He told me that in his days at Boston Consulting Group, just before he was to present concerning a client company, his BCG mentor said to him (I'm paraphrasing) he hoped Ken's briefing covered the last 30 years of background on their client company.

Ken had thought the five years he had looked at was "dramatic" but came to believe that to grasp the core of a business, you had to zoom out—and measure its history in decades.

Ken told me that story as background before he showed me a fascinating 60 year graph of IBM's progress.

Ken Keverian says both he and Ginni Rometty believe that vision depends on the object of the focus: "you can't define yourself around a product. Products come and go, they become mature and markets grow and shrink. So if you define your identity around your product or a series of products, you are destined not to survive 100 years.

"If you define yourself around clients, value and capability, constantly looking for the higher sources of value, then there's an ever increasing market. The challenge is it's constantly shifting out there."

Some have criticized IBM for simultaneously adding new products while eliminating old products. These critics believe this practice causes IBM to lose focus and to lack discipline, especially so regarding its core and customers. IBM would reply that it must have multiple visions: today's products and those of the future. Balancing them is not easy but is critical.

APPENDIX

IBM Isn't the Only One

IBM isn't the only company where big data and artificial intelligence will play prominent roles in the future. Because this book's topic is visions and visionaries, it's important to treat the relationship between vision and future. As noted earlier, vision has no presence in the future; it merely envisions the future in the present. How is that done?

All animals use data even if by senses, not minds. And we humans are barraged every day by increasingly more data every day. It's not just the cumulative effect adding more data each year. It's a growing population, more development and more data that's further enhanced by improved devices and methods for slicing and dicing data thereby creating geometrically more data and an unlimited potential for instantaneously communicating it. That not only expands the quantity of data but also the amount of non-factual data. Our minds have processed data with our imperfect algorithms in our underutilized brains forever. Today that's more challenging, and tomorrow who knows?

So what's the big deal, these days, about big data and algorithms? They apparently have been around forever. Today the uses of algorithms are meaningful in respect to when, why, and not just how they are used, relative to vision:

Algorithms to Reduce Risk:

This is what Bob Walter did to determine the likely timing of purchases, to gauge how long groceries and later drugs would last.

Algorithm to Increase Revenue:

Fred Smith redefined FedEx's raison d'etre from shipping packages to establishing customer reliance and faith. He used algorithms to do that.

Algorithms to Achieve or Maintain Visions:

Rick Waddell's vision of maintaining his beloved Northern Trust used traditional and not-so-traditional numerics to support and maintain the vision.

Algorithms from Which Visions Are Derived:

Rocky Wirtz used simple algorithms: the percentage of empty seats; comparables at other teams; the amount of debt he inherited versus cash flow; and his self-imposed limits for hobby costs.

Michael Jordan at Bat: A Legend, NOT

Sportscasters often refer to a player's feat as being the result of great athleticism, generally the ability to move well, quickly and easily. Athleticism is one skill set or discipline. There's also the other discipline—the skill of applying athleticism to a particular sport.

Michael Jordan, arguably the best basketball player ever, certainly had athleticism. But when he took leave from the Bulls to try out for Major League Baseball, athleticism aside, he lacked the second discipline and couldn't make the team.

Wayne Gretzky, perhaps the greatest hockey player, coined the oft-quoted key to his success: "I skate to where the puck is going to be, not where it has been."

That's a great quote. Unfortunately, while it expresses a goal (no pun intended), it doesn't explain how to achieve it. A puck would come off an opponent's stick at any of several angles, depending on the puck's angle coming toward his stick, the direction the opponent was skating, the angle of his swing and the surface of the ice. NHL players might get to the point of gauging that angle (the trend) but not be able to accurately discern the speed at which it travels (the pattern). Without knowing the speed, it's difficult to guess where or how your path will intersect that of the puck.

Keep that in mind as you develop your skills. And don't be afraid to bring on board people whose skills complement your own, who bring discipline expertise that when combined with your discipline expertise are the equivalent of 1+1=3. That's best achieved where one has both the equivalent of athleticism and particular applied skills.

How do you find such a person? First, be sure you've objectively determined your capabilities, the strength of your discipline. Then, you'll be better able to determine the other disciplines you'll need. I suggest you don't start with the person. You start with the raw discipline. Eventually, you must gauge the person—personality, work ethic, honesty, sociability and the like. That's screening not targeting. Then the process requires separating the discipline expertise, just one of the person's elements, from all the others.

Bob Walter hired Doug Linton, based on his mastery of his discipline, algorithmic science. Then Bob converted his own knowledge of retail, his customers' industry category, to the discipline of investment, which he had determined to be the best common denominator discipline. Voila! Retail meets algorithms at the stock exchange. Vision accomplished!

That's what I meant by "orchestrating the combination [of the skills/disciplines] of others." All too often, I've watched leaders identify the people with the needed disciplines and successfully attract them to their company, only to see the project fail, because they didn't understand or weren't sensitive to each other's disciplines, i.e. they effectively spoke different languages.

I'm not a musician, but I know that the sheet music isn't identical for all the musicians in an orchestra. I dare say, some would have problems playing as part of the orchestra if given another musician's sheet music.

The conductor becomes the translator, the interpreter. So must business leaders.

You can't stop doing your homework when you find, nor even when you land, your needed discipline expert. Follow-up homework is incumbent on good business leaders to bring all parties onto the same plain, using the same playbook.

Of course, there is an additional dimension. The leader must explain the vision and the goal, how the disciplines must be combined, what the combination is to accomplish and why that's necessary for successfully converting the vision to reality.

Read My Lips

President G.H.W. Bush used that phrase while running for president. It helped him win, but then helped him lose reelection because he had to backtrack and raise taxes. But as a great leader, he understood the need to make his vision and strategies clear and memorable.

Vision is not the same as strategies any more than strategy is the same as tactics.

There is a likely fictional old story from World War II. German U-boats were terrorizing Allied ships. Ally admirals gathered around a simulated Atlantic Ocean table to collaborate and plan. A British admiral suggested a solution: heat the ocean to boiling, and all the submarines will rise to the surface. A Yankee admiral asked how it was possible to do that, to which the Brit replied: "Ah, that's tactics; I only deal with strategy."

Carrying that story forward: the goal was to eliminate the U-boat threat; the vision was to gain Germany's unconditional surrender.

Ruth Bigelow's vision was for more, ever-more, Americans to drink Bigelow tea. Her goal was to move to a venue where her product was more scalable.

Her son, David, willingly and successfully attempted to overcome the shortcomings and inefficiencies of small gift shops by working harder. He likely maximized the gift stores' potential but was up against the tea strainer ceiling of gift stores. He feared a double-barreled calamity if they entered supermarkets.

Ruth's vision could not become a reality using David's goals and strategies, no matter how successfully he deployed them. Ruth's vision required a different goal. For Bigelow that proved to be a super market.

George Stephen's vision was for Weber to be the preeminent barbecue grill brand. His son Jim's goal was to develop a gas grill better than competitors' grills, in case gas grills overcame charcoal grills in the marketplace.

Employing a reverse engineering approach to copy the competition followed a traditional methodology for quickly catching up with competitors. However, a me-too approach was inconsistent with George's vision and Jim's goal. To be the preeminent brand meant being better than the others. Reverse engineering's inherent goal: to be the same as others, by definition, negates being better. So Jim threw out the others' grills. Instead, they reexamined the Weber charcoal grill that had become the preeminent charcoal grill and had the quality that he needed to produce a superior model.

Visions generally entail a large emotional component. Over time, rational justifications support the vision; they also may prevent proper analysis of the vision's continued viability, as well as whether the goals continue to be the best ways of achieving the visions.

In the heat of starting or building a business, when the focus on day-to-day tasks overwhelms, someone must step back and determine whether the hard work, dedication and persistence are consistent with the vision.

In start-ups, entrepreneurs must be that arbiter and monitor. When the entrepreneur starts to micromanage or worse yet be the jack-of-all-trades and the master-of-none, it becomes difficult to find the time or more important the brain space to analyze the trend pattern and determine whether and how fast it is moving toward the vision.

More established companies have multiple layers of management. They often succumb to the tendencies of leaders to surround themselves with "yes people" or to encourage, indeed not to discourage, such approving behavior. The result can be blind marches toward short or intermediate goals or misperceived visions and goals. The results become similar to the Yogi Berra line: "We're making good time but we're lost."

How to avoid such a result? The leaders must be clear about their visions and must clearly explain the visions to their followers. In *Invent Reinvent Thrive* I told the Starbucks stories. I asked CEO Howard Schultz how such a superb salesman had so many potential investors pass on what became one of the best start-up investments ever. His answer, half joking: "I guess I introduced a coffee too strong for Americans' tastes, put it in a paper cup and charged more than they were accustomed to paying."

Howard simply failed to explain his brilliant vision. His vision has little to do with coffee; it had to do with the club-like atmosphere he gave clients. He gave them a 1,000 piece jigsaw puzzle without the picture on the box cover.

The lesson: followers can't read a leader's mind, only his or her lips. Ruth Bigelow's vision was explicit and expressed. Jim Stephen manifested his father's vision by "throwing out" the competitors' grills they had been reverse-engineering. Keith Williams issued weekly memos to all employees to be sure there was no question about his vision.

Ross Perot's visions were always expressed clearly and visually. Those of you who saw his half-hour TV commercials during his run for U.S. president remember his use of visual aids. And remember his verbal description, every Sunday, of his vision for the raw land he had bought. It may have made his kids' eyes roll, as they sat in the car's back seat, but no one doubted the clarity of his visions.

The lesson is worth repeating as expanded by Perot's action: followers can't read a leaders mind only his or her lips, and nothing embeds actions in followers' minds, whether your employees or children or both, than repetition.

The Base Is a Pyramid's Foundation

Ancient Egyptians designed the pyramids in a fashion that has withstood millennia. Starting at the pyramid's apex point, each level rests on the foundation of the next level down.

In business, tactics rest on strategies, which rest on goals that in turn rest on the ultimate foundation of visions. A great leader has many functions, but one of the most important is to develop a clear vision.

We've already discussed the need for the business leaders' visions to be clear and properly communicated. Leaders must also keep their focus on the vision. If all the levels of an ancient pyramid had slipped off the pyramid base, it's unlikely we'd know of pyramids today. Egyptian leaders kept an eye on the progress. They were there to assure that each stone was properly set in place to gain maximum advantage of its foundation. Remember the upside-down organization chart lesson Rick Waddell learned from Wes Christopherson (chapter 9). So too, business leaders must keep their eyes on implementation, to be certain they are consistent with and supportive of the visions.

Visionaries' Special Problems With Naysayers

All successful business leaders had naysayers along the way. When naysayers argue with leaders' tactics, it may actually be a more fundamental disagreement over strategies or goals. Similarly, a strategy naysayer, may not comprehend the leaders' goals at all. Such naysaying can be helpful, if it spurs the leader to do better homework with a goal of knowing more than the naysayer knows. The ability of a naysayer to be meaningfully helpful is in fact greatest at the tactics level, where approaches are more concrete and thus discernible. That ebbs as one moves up the chain, to strategy, to goals. However, such a helpfulness becomes less accurate, less likely to prove helpful and successful, as one gets to the vision aspect.

Earlier I wrote about the business leader's need to describe his or her business vision clearly. However, I firmly believe our most important sense is hearing. Listening is often the key to vision. We learn far more by listening than by talking. Interesting fact: "listen and silent: two words with the same letters. It must be more than coincidence."

The odds are that one who is naysaying your vision doesn't really understand your vision. Listening carefully and learning what the naysayer understands can help you improve how you articulate your vision, as well as help prevent your following the naysayer to your detriment, when in fact the naysayer doesn't even get it, doesn't really understand what your vision really is.

(IQ+EQ)<UQ

Most of you know that IQ stands for Intelligence Quotient, a measure of one's intellect, and EQ for Emotional Intelligence, the measure of one's ability to handle interpersonal relationships. UQ is my creation. It stands for Understanding Quotient, a measure of how well you comprehend all aspects of a finding or situation.

I'm not a mathematician and don't even play one on TV. I do, however, believe that UQ can be greater in importance than IQ and EQ combined.

All too often I watch those with high IQ or EQ or even both become complacent. It's much like the company that captures its market. Both seem to succumb to the arrogance of riches. No matter how smart one is, lacking all the facts, or improperly discerning what are truly facts, or failing to really understand the facts leads inevitably to bad conclusions and decisions. And that generally leads to failure. Of course, even one with a bad UQ can win over competitors with worse UQs. That's simply is a bad way to plan and run your business, unless you're in the casino business.

Create Your Own Vision Calisthenics

You have the point, of course. But how can you create your own exercises? Start by deciding what traits and skills need improvement. Here are some examples, with an easy to remember acrostic:

Studious Homework: finding and understanding facts and separating logical and emotional components.

Comprehension: be sure both you and others understand your vision.

Objectivity: cold, calculating measure of your and others' business assets and liabilities.

Realism: measuring realistic prospects of achieving visions and goals.

Elegant Fit: aligning suitable goals, strategies and tactics suitable for and aligned with the vision.

Then pick, one at a time, and develop your own exercises to develop that particular capability. For example, to develop your homework, don't just read an article, work at determining what are facts and what are something else.

THE VISION THING

Visionarie$ Are Made Not Born

Business visionaries certainly have both genetic and environmental influences. I don't pretend to have the magic recipe for those ingredients. Since I doubt that anyone does, I suggest: It's too late to choose your parents, so focus on what you can affect.

A Life Devoted to Visualizing Business Visionaries

▼▼▼▼▼▼▼▼▼▼▼▼▼

E arly on, my understanding of a visionary's process was foggy. I remember, decades ago, talking with "Pop" Ibasfalean, the founder and owner of Cortez Marina in Florida. Pop was raised in a landlocked European community, yet conceived of and built, with his own hands, the largest marina south of Tampa on Florida's West Coast. "How did you conceive of this?" I remember asking Pop. His reply, "I just looked out there and saw the marina. Then all I had to do was build it." Today, I'm uncertain whether he saw it as a "gift from God," or simply lacked the ability or desire to articulate the process. What I do know for sure: he was not terribly different from other visionaries I've known.

Over a period of several decades, I have been fortunate to represent, interview and know thousands of business visionaries. Certainly the quality and value of their visions vary considerably, from extremely impactful to less so, from industry-wide breadth to isolated niche, from long-lasting to brief duration. For some, the vision resulted in its conversion to wealth for the visionary or for the visionary's backers and/or colleagues.

Other visionaries couldn't—or just didn't—take advantage of their visions. (Sometimes, others, aware of an idle vision, used it.)

Such passive visionaries are seen much as the unobserved tree falling in the forest, in that they don't get to enjoy the trappings of success. That does not negate the existence of or even the value of the unexploited vision.

During my two decades of teaching at the Kellogg School of Management at Northwestern University, I was delighted to expose students to great business visionaries.

My students and I are forever grateful to those visionaries who gave us their valuable time. Many of those visionaries as well as other visionaries I knew or worked with agreed to be interviewed for my books, *Entrepreneurs Are Made Not Born, Invent Reinvent Thrive* and *Visionarie$ are Made Not Born.*

I also thank clients from my law practice, at the Chicago firm, Shefsky & Froelich which I founded there in 1970. The firm was recently merged into the 130-year-old regional law firm, Taft, Stettinius and Hollister. This is a Cincinnati, Ohio firm whose best known partner was Senator Robert Taft who co-authored the Taft Hartley Law. In effect, Shefsky & Froelich became the Illinois branch of the Taft firm.

I thank as well those I served as a consultant over the past 20 years. These clients included numerous large family enterprises, lots of start-ups and other businesses of all types.

Those clients gave me the opportunity to observe the development of their businesses: to watch as their visions were formulated, developed and pursued to fruition. My observations of these clients were unstrained by the inevitable subsequent filters of selective recall.

My insight is not merely as observer and external advisor. My own visions led to my founding a new kind of law firm that focused on securities and tax law and also a Center for Family Enterprises (at the Kellogg School) and a sports professionals organization (the Sports Lawyers Association). All have proved notably successful. They required vision, if you will. The last defied the conventional wisdom that sports counsel were not worthy of a separate category of lawyering. That association is 2,000 members strong today worldwide. It has given prestige to a field that had been rife with raucous "Show Me The Money" pedantry and some unprincipled team owners who even hired goons to thwart fair-minded negotiation with top athletes. On those and other problems the Sports Lawyers Association proved helpful.

In addition, I have lectured, consulted and done business in numerous countries around the world.

Visions are affected by many factors one of which is certainly national and ethnic culture. What I have learned from and about each culture also helps me deal better with those from other cultures. For example, while teaching a course on entrepreneurship at Keio University in Japan, I learned more about how the Japanese culture made my students reticent to speak out in class.

That uniquely Japanese experience taught me to seek underlying causes for communications problems, such as where American family business people are communications challenged.

I relate these facts to explain my perspective and to establish my credibility with you the reader so that you are better able to deal with what I present in this book.

I believe my perspective is unique in combining global experience representing and helping business visionaries. My global research focused on business visionaries about whom I have written books and articles. Their history formed the basis for my lecturing worldwide. I feel this will serve you well.

It's also important for you to understand the reasons for my transitioning 20 years ago from partner in my law firm into consulting and education. I continue "Of Counsel" to the post-merger law firm. Some legal clients had commented that they valued my guidance regarding business perspectives as much as my legal skills. Indeed, one told me that she viewed all lawyers as fungible but felt bound to me because of my business advice.

Whatever the value of my assistance to clients, I rarely influenced visions. In fact I claim no credit for their visions. The visionary inspirations were invariably their own.

I did, however, recognize early on that I had to understand the derivation, nature and development of my clients' visions, in order to best contribute to what followed.

Was it obvious to me that I worked with or interviewed business visionaries? Of course. At appropriate times, I even referred to them as visionaries. I didn't bother to explain the term. Who would need explanation that Howard Schultz (Starbucks), James Sinegal (Costco), Maxine Clark (Build-A-Bear), Jay Pritzker (Hyatt Hotels) and Kay Koplovitz (USA Network), were business visionaries? After all, everyone knows a business visionary when they see one. Right?

But recently, it struck me that the concept—business visionary—needed more attention, further study and analysis, to help people better understand visionaries and, if desired, to emulate them. That led to this book, *Visionarie$ Are Made Not Born*.

Lloyd E. Shefsky

ACKNOWLEDGEMENTS

I n contemplating who deserves mention here, I am overwhelmed and humbled. So many have influenced and assisted in numerous and important ways. Space limitations preclude full explanation and appreciation; each could be the subject of a full story. To those neglected by an imperfect memory, my apologies for the oversight which does not in any way reflect my feelings.

First and foremost, my thanks to the people I interviewed:

- David Abney, CEO of UPS;

- Cindi Bigelow—CEO and granddaughter of the founder of Bigelow Tea;

- David and Eunice Bigelow—parents of Cindi Bigelow (David is former CEO of Bigelow Tea);

- James Covert—Former Secret Service agent, Founder and CEO of Security Link;

- Ken Keverian—Senior V.P. Corporate Strategy of IBM;

- Kay Koplovitz—Founder of USA Network;

- Ross Perot—founder of EDS (sold to GM), founder of Perot Systems (sold to Dell), independent candidate for U.S. President;

▶ Ross Perot, Jr.—Founder & Chairman of Hillwood Real Estate Development and biggest inland port in U.S., Former Chairman of Perot Systems;

▶ Sarah Catherine Perot—Daughter of Ross Perot, Jr. and Law Student;

▶ Marc Schulman—CEO of Eli's Cheesecake;

▶ Fred Smith – Founder & CEO of Federal Express;

▶ James Stephen—Former CEO and son of founder of Weber-Stephen, manufacturer of Weber BBQ grills;

▶ Anthony Terlato, former CEO and Chair of Terlato Wines;

▶ William Terlato—CEO of Terlato Wine Group;

▶ Frederick Waddell, CEO & Chairman of The Northern Trust Company.

▶ Robert Walter—Founder and former CEO of Cardinal Health;

▶ Eitan Wertheimer—Former CEO of Iscar, which he sold to Berkshire Hathaway;

▶ Keith Williams—CEO of Underwriters Laboratories;

▶ Rocky Wirtz—CEO and grandson of the founder of Wirtz Corporation, owner of the Chicago Blackhawks NHL team, and Wirtz Beverage Group and Wirtz Realty Corporation;

All are extraordinary in accomplishment and willingness to open and share so that others might benefit. Hopefully, this book justifies their trust in me.

Also, my appreciation to the following people who facilitated contacting, obtaining, scheduling and conducting the interviews:

Tony Agnone; George Bennett; Bill Bryant; Liz Cerda; Sara Cody; Elizabeth Corley; Karen D'Annibale; Elaine Gavoli; Katie Jenkins; Roni Kampf; Cindy Krch; John McClure; Patti Meadows; John Miller; Toni Morgan; Paige Myrlin; David Paulison; Sally Polaskey; Hedy Ratner; Bob Ruxin; Virginia Webster; and Sally Wolff.

Assisting me with research, clerical matters, layout and other arrangements were: my very able assistant, Julie Swidler, as well as Carol Zsolnay, Dana Levitt-Geraci, Dawn Steirn and Paul Romer; and I am deeply indebted to Robert Metz for provoking and challenging my thoughts and style and to Bill White with whom I commiserated over the art and science of authoring and the challenge of publishing.

Many thanks to the extremely talented and creative brand and design expert, Ron Swidler and his colleagues at the The Gettys Group, Angelica Acebedo-Frint, Adam Frint and Shane Bender, who helped with designing the book jacket, as well as creating links to the videos and my web site, formatting, branding and so much more.

Thanks also to those who supported my visions over the years: the members of my law firm, Shefsky and Froelich, now Taft Stettinius and Hollister; my clients, first as a lawyer and later as consultant, whose challenges continually tested and expanded my capabilities and from whom I continually learned; the board, members and successor presidents of the Sports Lawyers Association; Deans Jacobs, Jain and Blount of the Kellogg School and especially Professor John Ward, my partner at the Center for Family Enterprises. My Kellogg students over the years probably have no idea how important they were to the development of my concepts. And sincere appreciation to the class guests, over a span of two decades, who gave so much of their precious time and who bravely exposed their inner thoughts to help my students and from whom I learned so much.

As for the book itself, when all is said and done, the buck stops here: any mistakes are solely mine and any slights are truly unintentional.

AUTHOR'S REQUEST

I hope you enjoyed *Visionarie$ Are Made Not Born*. Please tell your friends and colleagues. Remember to write a review on your favorite book seller's website, expressing your appreciation of the quality of the work and the usefulness of my book to you as a reader.

Simply find the book on your favorite book seller's website and scroll down to where you see "Write a customer review."

INSTRUCTIONS FOR ACCESS TO BONUS MATERIAL

▼▼▼▼▼▼▼▼▼▼▼

Dear Readers,

E-Book readers of *Visionarie$ Are Made Not Born* can touch hyperlinks throughout the book and view video excerpts from the extraordinary interviews. In this hardcover book, these appear in brackets, e.g., [Wirtz 1].

I want you to have similar access to those videos as you read this hard-copy book.

The process is simple:

1. Go to my website: www.lloydshefsky.com

2. This website will guide you to register as a Special Reader

3. Where it asks for your Special Offer ID, fill in your first and last initials followed by the following number: 22113142 (for example, in my case it would be, LS22113142)

4. You will be asked for your email address and to create a password, which you can use to revisit the videos as you read the book.

5. The website will then direct you on how to view the videos.

Many thanks.

Regards, Lloyd

lloyd@lloydshefsky.com

INDEX